NO SERENITY HERE

An Anthology of African Poetry
in Amharic, English, French, Arabic and Portuguese

这里不平静

非洲诗选

Edited by Phillippa Yaa de Villiers
Isabel Ferrin-Aguirre
Xiao Kaiyu

主编
［南非］菲丽帕·维利叶斯
［德国］伊莎贝尔·阿闺热
［中国］萧开愚

世界知识出版社

Preface

Welcome to our world, a world created by 26 poets from 12 countries on the continent of Africa! A world that is under construction, filled with noise: the rumble of diggers and building machinery, in urban spaces Chinese-manufactured boom-boxes blare out jazz and indigenous pop music. If you have the ears to hear, the landscape exhales the song of birds, the calls of animals and the ancient drumbeat of African cultural traditions.

Initially, African poetry was ritualistic and anonymous, that is to say, within those early communities poets and storytellers who had a gift with the language and a richness of idiom were celebrated within those communities, Authorship was not a priority until words were captured in books. Z. Pallo Jordan, South Africa's former Minster of Arts and Culture, in his foreword to his father AC Jordan's seminal Tales from Southern Africa writes: "The ethos of traditional society was enshrined in an oral legal, religious, and literary tradition through which the community transmitted from generation to generation its customs, values and norms. The poet and the storyteller stood at the centre of this tradition, as the community's chroniclers, entertainers, and collective conscience." [Tales from Southern Africa, translated and retold by A.C. Jordan, University of California Press 1973] Because orality was dynamic and improvised and relied on the audience's participation, the storyteller's creativity includes facilitating the communal voice, what Jordan refers to as "the collective genius". For this reason writers like Keorapetse Kgositsile say: "Poetry will survive without me. It was here long before me and it will continue long after me."

We wanted to include traditional oral poetry, so that readers could get a sense of the history captured in the idiom of working songs and women's songs, and more recently, struggle or resistance songs, because this, for us, *is also classical literature*. Many traditional poems have been translated and recorded in anthologies published by western houses like Penguin, Jonathan Cape and Faber and Faber. We were unable to get the rights to republish these poems because of the bureaucracy of these institutions – but we hope the essence of these early texts has informed our choice and you can still 'feel' the African tradition through the voices of contemporary poets.

Kgositsile's *In the Naming* explores the emotional results of the colonial practice of renaming African settlements. Rhini is the African name for a place where people have lived since time began, and Grahamstown is the name of a relatively recent military base and colonial town. It is the same physical place, but experienced entirely differently by two different sets of citizens, English speaking and Xhosa or Afrikaans speaking, white and black. This is a portrait of a town, a microcosm of South Africa and its historical contradictions, and captures the essence of some of those contradictions for the whole continent.

Kofi Anyidoho gives voice to loss of identity, language and culture and tradition as he charts the journey of a twin brother who is seduced into the easy promises of the West. Song of Twin Brother was composed in honour of master poet Kofi Awonoor:

> ...*And here I am today,*
> *Holding on to Grandfather's sinking boat*
> *While Atsu my Twin Brother*

Floats on air in Jumbo Jets
And stares into the skies
And dreams of foreign ports...

Many of the poems that you will read here carry the imprint of the poet's mother tongue: there are close to 2000 indigenous languages spoken on the continent. The colonial experience and slavery depleted Africa of resources like gold, copper, platinum and oil but also the languages and cultures that ensure social cohesion and historical continuity. At the same time, the strange benefit of having languages like French, English, Portuguese and Arabic imposed was that it allowed fellow language users across the continent and further into the world to engage with African thought.

And African thought is vibrant and varied: from Tolu Ogunlesi (Nigeria) and Stanley Kenani (Malawi), to Obodimmo Oha (Nigeria), Dorian Haarhoff (South Africa,) Tania Tome (Moçambique), Beaven Tapureta (Zimbabwe) and Keamogetsi Molapong (Namibia) and Alemu Tebeje Ayele (Ethiopia), we explore the human condition via their hearts and minds. We recreate the fireside of oral poetry with the inclusion of three internationally renowned performance poets, TJ Dema, Lebo Mashile and Shailja Patel.

You might say that this anthology is hopelessly inadequate, when there are more than 50 countries in the continent, each with its highly respected canon of indigenous literature we have only 26 poets! This is not a definitive work, it is a handful of seeds from which we invite you to feed your curiosity. This anthology was created in a desire to offer an experience of Africa through poetry to the Chinese people: in a celebratory spirit Xiao Kaiyu was asked to throw a party for African poets, Isabel Ferrin-Aguirre was given the task of sending out the invitations, and I was asked for names.

South Africa, as most recently liberated country in Africa, is also the most industrialized and the economic powerhouse of the sub-continent. With its history of racism and resistance, South Africa is a microcosm of the world, becoming a home to Europeans and Asians, who daily commit themselves to the task of creating a society based on values of equality and non-racialism. Africa, already diverse, now is home to people from the whole planet, and this is reflected in the choice of poets. For these reasons, and also because South Africans were more accessible, there are more of them featured in the anthology.

Together with Isabel and Kaiyu, we decided on the order of the poems and the journey through the pages. We invite you to listen to our elders, the Nobel Laureate Wole Soyinka (Nigeria), South Africa's National Poet Laureate Keorapetse Kgositsile, Ghana's Kofi Anyodoho, Chirikure Chirikure from Zimbabwe, Shabbir Banoobhai and James Matthews from South Africa, and younger voices like Nii Ayikwei Parkes (Ghana), and Hama Tuma (Ethiopia). We introduce you to the unsung co-creators of literature: the giants Ama Ata Aidoo (Ghana), Fatima Naoot (Morocco), Veronique Tadjo (Côte d'Ivoire), Makhosazana Xaba (South Africa), Joyce Chigiya and Amanda Hammar both from Zimbabwe.

Music is one of Africa's major exports, and the proximity of poetry to song is heard over and over again in the cadences of the poems that are gathered here. The poems are arranged around broad themes of:

The internet has played a major role in collecting and compiling this work, which speaks to the technological fluency of African writers. As barriers dissolve, the entire planet becomes the setting for the ritual, the storyteller's fire, the dance of words in which all are invited to see themselves reflected. You will not find serenity between these pages, you will find voices struggling, laughing, weeping, voices that are alive, roaring and whispering as they enrich the world's song by adding their voices.

Phillippa Yaa de Villiers

Johannesburg, 10 May 2010

序一

欢迎来到我们这个世界，一个由非洲大陆12个国家26个诗人所组成的世界！一个正在施工的喧嚣的世界：挖掘机和建筑机械的隆隆声，市镇里中国造的便携式收录机放出的刺耳的爵士乐和本地流行音乐，如果你听得见，风景中还传出鸟的歌唱，动物的叫唤，以及非洲文化传统幽邈的鼓点。

最初的非洲诗歌是仪式性和不署名的，也就是说，在早期的社群里，诗人和故事讲述者语言出众、语汇丰富，受到他们社群的尊崇，但在这些语言进入书本之前，作者的概念并不被优先考虑。Z.帕劳·乔丹，前南非艺术文化部长，为他父亲AC乔丹具有开创性的《来自南非的故事》撰写的前言中写道："传统社会的精神被口头的律法、宗教和文学传统所尊崇，通过这个传统，人们一代接着一代传承它的习俗、价值观和规范。诗人和故事讲述者作为这个社群的纪年者，表演者和集体的良心，就站在这个传统的中心。"（《来自南非的故事》，A.C.乔丹译述，加利福尼亚大学出版社，1973）由于口头表达是动态的、即兴的，有赖于听众的参与，故事讲述者的创造力就包括发出集体的声音，即乔丹提到的"集体性天赋"。正因为如此，凯奥拉佩策·考斯尔等作家才说："诗歌的生存不需要我。它在我之前很早就存在了，也将在我之后长久存在下去。"

我们本来也想收入传统的口头诗歌，这样读者就能从劳动歌谣、妇女歌曲，以及晚近的挣扎反抗的歌曲里捕获一种历史感，因为这对我们来说，也是古典文学。很多传统诗歌已被翻译和收入一些选集，由企鹅、乔纳森·开普、费伯和费伯等西方的出版社出版，但因为这些机构的官僚作风，我们无法得到再版这些诗的许可。然而，我们希望这些早期文本的精髓已经贯穿了我们的选择，你能从当代诗人的声音中仍然"感觉到"非洲的传统。

考斯尔的《在命名中》探索了对非洲殖民地重新命名的殖民做法的情感后果。利尼是一个非洲地名，人们自古就在那里生活，格雷厄姆斯敦则是一个新兴的军事基地和殖民城市。这两个名字所指的是同一个地方，两组不同的人群却经验迥异：讲英语的和讲科萨语或南非荷兰语的，白种人或黑种人。这是一幅城市的画像，是南非及其历史矛盾的一个缩影，它抓住了属于整个大陆的某些矛盾的本质。

科菲·阿尼多赫谈到了身份、语言、文化和传统的丧失。他记述了被西方的廉价承诺所诱惑的一对孪生兄弟的旅程。《双胞胎兄弟之歌》一诗是为纪念诗歌大师科菲·阿沃诺而作的：

> ……今天我在这里，
> 抓住我祖父下沉的小船
> 而我的双胞胎兄弟阿特苏
> 飘浮在天上在喷气客机中
> 凝视着天空
> 梦想着外国的港口……

这里的很多诗歌都打上了诗人的母语的烙印：这片大陆上有接近2000种本土语言在使用。殖民经历和奴隶制耗尽了非洲的资源，像金、铜、铂和石油，更耗尽了确保社会凝聚力和历史连续性的语言文化。另一方面，从外部强加来的语言，如法语、英语、葡萄牙语、阿拉伯语，却很诡异地带来了好处，它能让非洲大陆进而全世界使用这些语言的人介入非洲的思想。

而非洲的思想是充满活力和多种多样的：从陶鲁·欧冈勒斯（尼日利亚）、斯坦利·克那尼（马拉维），到奥波多迪玛·奥哈（尼日利亚）、多利安·哈尔霍夫（南非）、塔尼娅·托麦（莫桑比克）、比温·塔普莱塔（津巴布韦）、齐莫格茨·莫拉庞（纳米比亚）、阿莱姆·特伯热·艾尔（埃塞俄比亚），我们通过他们的心灵与头脑来考查人类的境况。通过收入三位国际知名的表演诗人，TJ迪玛、勒布·马希尔和莎尔遮·佩特尔，我们重新点燃了口头诗歌的篝火。

你可能会说这个选本严重不足：非洲大陆有50多个国家，每个国家都有其令人尊敬的本土文学经典，而我们仅收入26位诗人！这部诗选并非终极选本，而是一把培养你的好奇心的种子。这个选本的目的是通过诗歌给中国人民提供一点非洲经验：大家提议萧开愚为非洲诗人举办一个派对，伊莎贝尔·阿闰热发请柬，而我来提供人选。

作为最晚解放的非洲国家，南非是非洲次大陆最工业化的经济强国。带着它种族主义和抵抗运动的历史，南非是世界的一个缩影，它正在成为欧洲人和亚洲人的家园，他们每天都承担着重任，以创造一个基于平等和非种族主义价值观的社会。非洲本已多姿多彩，现在更是来自整个星球的人们的栖所，这也反映在诗人的挑选上。出于这些原因，也因为南非诗人更容易接触到，所以这本诗选中他们也展示得更多一些。

与伊莎贝尔和开愚一道，我们确定了诗人的顺序和书的编排方式。我们邀请你聆听我们的长者，诺贝尔奖获得者沃莱·索因卡（尼日利亚）、南非的国家桂冠诗人凯奥拉佩策·考斯尔、加纳的科菲·阿尼多赫、津巴布韦的齐里克热·齐里克热、南非的沙比尔·巴努海和詹姆斯·马修斯，以及像奈伊·阿伊克维·帕克斯（加纳）和阿玛·图玛（埃塞俄比亚）等更年轻的声音，我们也要向你介绍尚未得到足够赞誉的文学世界的共同创造者：巨匠阿玛·阿塔·艾杜（加纳）、法提玛·纳乌特（摩洛哥）、伏罗尼克·塔乔（科特迪瓦）、马克霍萨萨纳·萨巴（南非）和同样来自津巴布韦的乔伊斯·齐基娅与阿曼达·哈玛。

音乐是非洲的一项主要出口产品，诗与歌的亲缘性可以从收集于此的诗里一再听到。这些诗是根据以下宽泛的主题来安排的：

1.风景和变化
2.身份、历史和语言
3.压迫和反抗
4.爱
5.希望与前途

在本书的收集和编辑过程中，互联网起到了重要作用，这也说明了非洲作家的技术熟练程度。随着交流的障碍被打破，整个星球都为仪式，故事讲述者的篝火，以及词语的舞蹈而设，在这里，所有人都被邀请，去观看从中映出的他们自身。在这些书页里你将感受不到平静，你将听到挣扎的、大笑的、哭泣的声音，这些声音生机勃勃，或怒吼，或低语，所有声音的叠加丰富了这首世界之歌。

菲丽帕·维利叶斯
约翰内斯堡，2010年5月10日

Introduction

Renowned artist Hu Xiangcheng is profoundly drawn to the literary, as well as the visual, arts. At an early age, he spent some time in Africa and to this day has a deep longing for it. Thus, he entrusted me with overseeing the editing and translation of an anthology of African poetry. With the help of Phillippa Yaa de Villiers, a poet from South Africa, and the German literary figure Isabel Ferrin Aguirre, we have come up with this work.

Phillippa has already addressed the process of selection in her own preface. What I wish to clarify here is that although the three of us collectively established the principles and parameters of selection, the final say in matters of editorial strategy was primarily in the hands of the two of them, especially Phillippa. I was proud to have been included in their deliberations. The accumulation of source material and selection of the poets and poems was also carried about by the two of them together. Whenever I would read the poems they would send, with their different languages and orientations, as well as the superb analyses they included with the poems, so many works and analyses, I would have a sense of fear: the vast subject matter confronted in African poetry, the profound meaning, the direct expression and the special admonition, would make me physically quiver as the poems shattered my expectations. In my previous involvement in various literary events in Europe I had come across some African poets who gave me the impression their works were adorned for momentary shock value. But this time, I was enveloped by an unsettling system of thought. It truly sank in to me that Africa is a part of the contemporary world with its imperiled environment, enigmatic relations, and its frayed psychology. No matter how innocent or unaffected, Africa is no exception to this. From the point of view of poetry per se, these works from an utterly different literary tradition are deeply inspiring. Not only does the subject matter strike a chord and the sentiments expressed in them are clearly apprehended; beyond the basic forms that poets from around the world share, they present all sorts of unique stylistic flourishes. One example is the construction of performative and ballad techniques as a powerful and direct way of opening the door.

I was able to secure poets with strong foreign language and poetic skills who happened to be available to do the translations. As the first reader, I believe they've done quite a handsome job, especially when it comes to the quality of their use of the Chinese language in conveying the meaning of the original and their ability to maintain a poetic character. Every poet has his or her own method of assessing poetry as it makes its debut in another language. With the results here in full view, the reader can get a taste of how different ways of achieving beauty vie with each other. Certain poems have different translations, and they are published here together.

The energetic support of the Jiang Nan Art and Design Foundation, which has been engaged in exploring how the interaction between the Neo-Confucianism, traditional arts and village society can be conceived for the contemporary world, and the Moonchu Foundation, have been a prerequisite for the success of this complex project. And for that I would like to express sincere gratitude. Finally, we would like to thank the insight and collegiality of World Affairs Press.

Xiao Kaiyu, Berlin, 26 June 2010

序二

艺术家胡项城先生对语言艺术作品也抱有深衷，他早年在非洲呆过一段，至今心驰神往，遂嘱托我来组织编译一本非洲诗选。我找到做国际文学活动的德国人伊莎贝尔(Isabel Ferrin Aguirre)，伊莎贝尔建议由南非诗人菲丽帕(Phillippa Yaa de Villiers)和我一道做编辑工作。

关于编选过程，菲丽帕已在她的序言里介绍过了。我要说明的是，编选的原则和范围虽由我们三人共同商定，最终成为编辑策略的建议则主要是她们二位尤其是菲丽帕贡献的。我为参与了讨论而感到骄傲。搜集资料、选择诗人和诗作的工作，也由菲丽帕和伊莎贝尔两位联合完成。每当读到她们传来的大量的不同语种和取向的诗歌作品以及她们所做的精湛评议，都让我震撼不已：非洲诗歌的广阔面对、幽深触及、直接表达和特别忠告，带着生理性的震颤，颠覆了我的期待。原先在欧洲种种文学活动中我结识过一些非洲诗人，他们像山间的点缀引起片刻诧异，而这次，我被一种不安的哲学覆盖了。我真实地体会到，非洲是我们这个环境告急、关系叵测和心理撕扯的当代世界的一部分，哪怕更多保有了天真但不是什么例外。从诗歌自身的角度讲，这些出自迥异的文化传统的作品令人振奋，它们不但内容结实，情感具有明晰的辨识度，而且在世界所有地区的诗人所共享的一些基本形式的基础上，奉献了多种特殊的形式因素，比如，塑造表演和说唱风格的强劲直贯的排闼法。

我邀请到诗艺和外文俱佳碰巧也抽得出空的几位诗人来做翻译，作为第一读者，我感觉他们翻得相当精彩，特别是在达意的时候保持住了汉语的质感和诗歌的性格。每位诗人对诗歌在另一门语言中登场的方式有自己的设计，这里把结果展示出来，读者可以看到不同的出彩法如何地斗艳。所以，个别诗作有了不同的翻译，这里一并发表。

致力于探索理学、传统工艺与乡镇社会形态如何在当代性的生活构想中交互发生作用的江南工艺社（Jiang Nan Art and Design foundation) 和梦周文教基金会（Moonchu foundation) 的鼎力支持，是完成这项复杂的工程的前提，在此诚挚地致谢。最后，感谢世界知识出版社的慧眼相识。

萧开愚
2010年6月26日于柏林

Acknowledgments

We would like to thank Monica Rorvik of Poetry Africa for her assistance in contacting poets, as well as Irene Staunton of Zimbabwe Poetry International. Internet sites such as *http://www.african-writing.com/nine/* and Poetry International *www.poetry-international.org*, as well as www.lyrikline.org and *http://famous-poetsandpoems.com/* also gave us access to some of our poets. We also read several anthologies in order to deepen our understanding of African Poetry, and if you are interested in learning more, we recommend the following titles:

- ❖ You Better Believe It (Penguin, 1973) ed. Paul Breman
- ❖ The Penguin Book of Modern African Poetry (Penguin 1998) edited by Gerald Moore and Ulli Beier
- ❖ Daughters of Africa (Jonathan Cape 1981) edited by Margaret Busby
- ❖ The Rattle Bag (Faber and Faber 1982) edited by Ted Hughes and Seamus Heaney
- ❖ The Heinemann Book of African Poetry in English (Heinemann, 1990) edited by Adewale Maja-Pearce
- ❖ Women writing Africa: this massive 4-volume set of writing is a project of the Feminist Press at City University of New York (2007)
- ❖ A Rain of Words. A bilingual Anthology of Women's Poetry in Francophone Africa (Virginia Press, 2009) edited by Irène Assiba d'Almeida
- ❖ Antilopenmond. Liebesgedichte aus Afrika (Peter

Hammer Verlag, 2002), edited by Peter Ripken / Véronique Tadjo.

We also gratefully acknowledge the friends who lent us books and spoke to us about this idea as it was busy coming to life, and the poets who lent their words to this volume.

感谢

《非洲诗集》的莫尼卡·罗维克和《津巴布韦国际诗集》的爱琳·斯道顿帮助我们联络到相关诗人。http://www.african-writing.com/nine/ 和 www.poetryinternational.org, 诗歌网站 www.lyrikline.org 和 http://famouspoetsandpoems.com/ 也向我们推荐了诗人。我们在此一并向上述个人与网站表示衷心感谢。与此同时,为了提高对非洲诗歌的欣赏,我们翻阅了一些文集。如各位读者有意对非洲诗歌作进一步的探讨,请参考如下材料:

《你最好相信》(企鹅,1973年),Paul Breman 编

《企鹅现代非洲诗集》(企鹅,1998年),Gerald Moore 和 Ulli Beier 编

《非洲的女儿》(Jonathan Cape 出版社,1981年),Margaret Busby 编

《嘎嘎袋》(Faber and Faber 出版社,1982年),Ted Hughes 和 Seamus Heaney 编

《Heineman 英语非洲诗集》(Heinemann 出版社,1990年),Adewale Maja-Pearce 编

《女作家笔下之非洲》:此四册之文集由纽约城市大学女权出版社出版,2007年

《文字之雨点:法语非洲女诗人双语诗集》(维吉尼亚出版社,2009年),Irene Assiba d'Almeida 编

《羚羊的世界:非洲情诗》(Peter Hammer 出版社,2002年),Peter Ripken 和 Véronique Tadjo 编

许多热心的朋友向我们提供相关书籍,并为我们出谋

划策，才促成了本集的应运问世。当然，没有非洲诗人的优美文字更没有本选集。我们无法一一点名，在此一并表示由衷的感谢。

Contents

目录

XXII

No serenity here

这里不平静

I Landscapes and Change

In this section poets reveal the landscape from which they write. Africa is a concept cloaked in intrigue, trauma, romance and drama but it is simply a geographically, culturally, and politically diverse continent, which has gone through centuries of relentless invasion and exploitation that has made it difficult if not impossible for Africans to define themselves. Who is listening? You, the reader, will hear the poets through their words, imagining and recreating their world.

I 风景和变化

在这一章，诗人用各自的语言来描述非洲风情。阴谋、创伤、浪漫和惊喜充肆着非洲大地；非洲同时又是一个从地理环境到文化和政治多元化的大陆。上百年来，非洲经历了入侵与剥削的蹂躏，连非洲人都不知如何给自己定位。谁在倾听？现在，请读者通过诗人的文字来感受其精神世界。

Somebody Decided to Build Lilongwe

Stanley Onjezani Kenani

Somebody decided to build Lilongwe
with its skyscrapers mingled with dust
with its prostitutes and beggars
gun-totting robbers, pick-pockets,
traffic jams and presidential motorcades.

Somebody decided to build Lilongwe
with its bars and nightclubs
with its immuno-deficiency viruses
its rapists, its sadists,
preachers and poachers.

Somebody decided to build Lilongwe
with its reserve(d) banks
with its Devil Street, its devils,
its mean-buses, its noise,
poise and call-boys.

Somebody decided to build Lilongwe
with its churches and curses
with its mournful dirges
its rural-like face
its mess.

Somebody decided to build chaos.

某人决定建造利隆圭

［马拉维］斯坦利·昂热扎尼·克那尼

某人决定建造利隆圭
用它混合泥尘的摩天楼
用它的娼妓和乞丐们
持枪的强盗们、扒手，
堵塞的交通和总统车队。

某人决定建造利隆圭
用它的酒吧和夜店
用它不免疫的病毒
它的强奸犯们、虐待狂们，
它的布道者和偷猎者。

某人决定建造利隆圭
用它准备（好）的银行
它的罪恶街，它的恶魔们，
它卑贱的小巴、它的噪声，
和泰然自若的应招男郎。

某人决定建造利隆圭
用它的教堂和咒语
用它悲恸的挽歌
用它乡下人的脸
用它的大便。

某人决定建造大混乱。

（张伟栋　译）

5

In the small hours

Wole Soyinka

Blue diaphane, tobacco smoke
Serpentine on wet film and wood glaze,
Mutes chrome, wreathes velvet drapes,
Dims the cave of mirrors. Ghost fingers
Comb seaweed hair, stroke acquamarine veins
Of marooned mariners, captives
Of Circe's sultry notes. The barman
Dispenses igneous potions
Somnabulist, the band plays on.

Cocktail mixer, silvery fish
Dances for limpet clients.
Applause is steeped in lassitude,
Tangled in webs of lovers' whispers
And artful eyelash of the androgynous.
The hovering notes caress the night
Mellowed deep indigo still they play.

Departures linger. Absences do not
Deplete the tavern. They hang over the haze
As exhalations from receded shores. Soon,
Night repossesses the silence, but till dawn
The notes hold sway, smoky
Epiphanies, possessive of the hours.

午夜

[尼日利亚] 沃莱·索因卡

蓝色透照灯，烟雾
在湿胶片和木釉上缭绕，
暗哑了铬色，罩住了丝绒幕布，
让镜中之穴昏暗。幽灵的手指
梳起海藻发型，轻抚栗色海员，希瑟女巫
肉感音符的俘虏，那美人鱼的纹理。服务生
端上火的饮料
梦游者一般，乐队演奏不停。

调酒师，银鱼
为帽贝顾客而舞。
掌声中浸透疲惫，
交织着恋人到处的低语
和阴阳人的假睫毛。
盘旋的音符爱抚着染透
靛蓝之夜他们仍在演奏。

送走滞留者。离场不会
让酒馆空虚。他们悬浮在烟雾之上
就像由退潮的海岸呼出。很快，
夜重归寂静，但直到天亮
音符都在飘荡，烟雾缭绕地
昭显着，宣示对时光的所有权。

This music's plaint forgives, redeems
The deafness of the world. Night turns
Homewards, sheathed in notes of solace, pleats
The broken silence of the heart.

音乐的哀叹宽恕，挽救了
世界的聋聩。夜晚显出
回家之意，披着慰藉的乐音的甲胄，揉皱
心的破碎的沉默。

（席亚兵　译）

Hungry streets

Amanda Hammar

These hungry pock-marked streets.
Potholes like piranhas, mouths
gaping open, ready to devour
cars, bicycles, bodies, whatever
might fall prey to their darkness.

The sunshine city has lost its sheen.
Its heart still beats insistently
but the gravel man has scraped out
its womb like a demon-surgeon.
Tomorrow no longer exists.

饥饿的大街

[津巴布韦] 阿曼达·哈玛

这些饥饿麻子般的大街。
凹坑像食人鲳的嘴大张
凝视着，准备吃光吞咽下
汽车、自行车、身体，任何
可能落入它们的黑暗的猎物。

这太阳城已经丢失了它的光辉。
它的心脏仍一而再地敲击
但是砾石人已经像恶魔外科医生般
刮出了它的子宫。
明天不再来临。

（张伟栋 译）

The art of listening

Tjawangwa Dema

The man on the balcony of the company's sixth floor
Says he knows the secret to life
Everyone laughs
Teething vultures biting at the wind
Tie askew
Everyone wishing they knew
What had freed him from the shackles they still clung to
He leaps
Back arched
Perfect stance
Arms wide
Phones flash
The earth shakes
The wind rises knowing there is nothing
Not a thing but it to break his fall
The man on the balcony
of the company's
sixth floor
Said he knew the meaning
of life
No one laughs
Not one
Not anymore

倾听的艺术

[博茨瓦纳] 贾旺娃·迪玛

在公司第六层楼阳台上的男人
说他知道通往生命的秘密
每一个人都笑
刚出牙的秃鹫对着风正咬
领带歪斜
每一个人都希望他们知道
是什么帮他摆脱了仍系着他们的镣铐
他跳
弓起背
姿势完美
双臂张开
话机闪灯
地面震动
风儿吹起知道什么也没有
什么也没有只有它中断了他的坠落
在公司
第六楼
阳台上的男人
说他知道生命
的意义
没有一个人笑
没有一个
再没有

（周伟驰　译）

Names

Tolu Ogunlesi

from up here the river is brown-
uniformed, a restless guard
dutifully separating the living

from the merely lively.
the living
is the green

of nature's turf. the lively
is everything else –
the toy cars raced by invisible hands,

the cages of steel & glass
where engines run
on blood, sweat & pride,

& the roads, clad in black;
aged referees running through
the impatient plans of the world.

diminished by desire, I succumb –
like every one of the restless rest –
to the riotous rhythms of these stands.

every now & then my gaze falls,

名字

[尼日利亚] 陶鲁·欧冈勒斯

从那里开始，河流是
穿棕色制服的躁动不安的
警卫，很尽责地将生者

和仅仅活着的分开。
生者
是大自然地皮上的

绿，活着的
是所有其他一切——
被看不见的手操控赛跑的玩具车，

钢和玻璃的牢笼，
那里的引擎运行于血、汗
和自尊心之上，

还有道路，镀成了黑色；
年迈的裁判在令人生厌的
世界平面图上来回奔跑。

被欲望缩减，我屈从于——
就像每一个躁动不安的休止符——
这些看台的暴乱的节奏。

间或我的凝视

like a gloomy shadow,
on one of the many hands

of fate, each painstakingly adding to the stone score
-board beyond the river's edge,
the names of yet more living dead.

像一块沮丧的阴影，落在
许多命运之手中的一只

每一只都将更多活死人的
名字，辛苦地添加到
河流边缘外的石头计分板上。

（丁丽英　译）

显像1　胡项城

（Appearance I　Hu Xiangcheng）

À mi-chemin

Véronique Tadjo

On ne part pas sans perdre du sang. Tu
reviens, le cœur plein de boones intentions.
Mais tes yeux parcourent la ville et tu tombes
de haut. Il faut tout reprendre à zero.

Tu veux toucher les autres, ceux à qui tu
pensais, là-bas, dans ton exil souterrain. Leur
peau est flétrie. Leurs visages se creusent de
rides assombries et la solitude se lit dans le
fond de leurs yeux.

Le retour, ah oui, le retour! Pour apprendre
que la mort était là avant toi et que les
oiseaux sont partis avec les dernières pluies.

En vérité, la solitude n'a pas de nom,
puisque'elle se cache dans les recoins de ton
corps. Elle se cache en suivant le chemin de
tes veines, la ligne de ta colonne vertébrale et
le marécage dense de ton esprit en éveil.

Interroge le miroir brisé, les fragments de ton
âme qui te dissent la vérité. Interroge la
cassure, l'éparpillement. Interroge, interroge,
jusqu'à l'épuisement.

在中途

［科特迪瓦］伏罗尼克·塔乔

只要血液尚存，我们就不会离去。
你回来了，心灵充满美好的愿望。
但是，你的眼睛在城市中逡巡，
然后从高处跌下，一切必须从零开始。

你想触碰那些你想念的人，
在那儿，在你地下的流放地。
他们的皮肤失去光泽。
他们的面孔凹陷下去。皱纹变得黯淡，
孤独显现在你眼窝深处。

归来，哦，是的，归来！
为了告知死亡在那里，在你的前面，
为了告知鸟儿们带着最后的雨水飞走了。

的确，孤独没有名字，
因为她藏匿在你身体的隐蔽处。
他藏匿在你的血管中，
你脊柱的线条和你警惕的神经的泥泞的沼泽中。

询问折起的镜子，
你灵魂的碎片告诉你真相。
询问裂缝，散落。询问，询问，
直到枯竭。

Car, il a fallu que nous naissions seuls. Il a
fallu trouver la lumière au bout du tunnel. Il
a fallu quitter la chaleur moite pour l'air sec
du dehors.

Tu as cassé le miroir
dans lequel tu te regardais
et tu ne te reconnais plus
Tu ignores jusqu'à
l'écriture de ton nom
et le son de ta voix

Tu ne connais
aucun chemin par cœur
Les détours te font peur
La ville a changé
plus vite que toi
Elle t'a filé
Entre les doigts

Oublie le souvenir
qui te retient
et t'empêche d'avancer
Le souvenir toujours
pour te dire
que les choses
ne sont plus les mêmes
que tes rêves

因为，我们原本应该独自出生。
原本应该发现隧道尽头的光线。
原本应该为了外面干燥的空气离开湿热。

你打碎了总是用来照自己的镜子
而且你不再认识自己
你不认识自己的名字
也不认识自己的声音

你不认识任何从心灵通过的道路
弯路让你害怕
城市改变的速度
比你更迅捷
她在手指之间
放开了你

忘记重新抓住你的回忆
并在前进中阻碍你
回忆总是
为了对你说
事情不再和你的梦相同
事情不再存活
在干燥的季节里

n'ont pas survécu
aus saisons sèches

Oublie qu'hier
tout était possible
et trouve une ligne à ta vie
un chemin à parcourir
qu'il pleuve ou qu'il vente
que tu aies
les larmes aux yeux
ou le sourire aux lèvres

Oublie
tes vieilles idées
tes souliers usés

Regarde-toi en face

La solitude
Ne t'a jamais quitté

As-tu remarqué que tes veines
sont à fleur de peau?
As-tu remarqué
Qu'elles gardent leur secret?

Il faut l'admettre
ton corps te trahit
déjà

24

忘记这里
一切都是可能的
并找到一条你生命的线
一条要走完的路
忘记下雨或者刮风
忘记你的眼睛中或许有泪水
忘记你的嘴唇上或许有微笑

忘记吧
你过去的想法
你破损的鞋子

正视你自己吧

寂寞
从来不曾离开过你

你注意到你的血管
是非常敏感的吗？
你注意到
她们保护着自己的秘密吗？

必须允许
你的身体流露真情
你的身体

qui ne suit plus tes passions
qui traîne les pieds
à tes derniers
rendez-vous

Comment veux-tu parler
de l'arbre et de ses fruits
quand les raciness se meurent
sous la terre malade?

Partir/revenir
ces allées et venues
de la vie
nous laissent fatigués
lassés que rien ne brise
l'exigence du temps

Tu es ici
tu es là-bas
Le monde est divisé
mais quand tu rassembles
tes amours
il n'y a pas de difference

Nous sommes des solitudes
éparses
sans jamais briser
les barrièrs

已经不再跟随你的感情
已经不再脚拖着地面走路
去往你最后的那些约会

你想怎么讲述
树木和它的果实
当根在生病的土地上死去?

离开/归来
这生命的来来去去
我们疲倦地离去
不打破时间的束缚

你在这里
你在那里
世界分裂
但是当你整理
你的感情
一切没有不同

我们是孤独
四处散落
却从不打破藩篱

Et il me dit
qu'il m'aime
et je dis
que je l'aime
mais je suis
toujours seule
depuis bien longtemps

Il te fait l'amour
et pourtant
tu n'oses pas
le toucher
son corps
comme un tam-tam
de guerre
Il te fait l'amour
Et pourtant tu ne sais pas
Quoi penser

Tu aurais aimé
toucher ses doigts
dans le fond
de ton lit
Tu aurais aimé
lui dire des mots
qui ne s'envolent pas
Ce que vous auriez pu être
pourquoi l'avez-vous fui?

他对我说
他爱我
我说
我爱他
但是我总是独自一人
从很久以前开始

他爱你
然而
你不敢触碰他
他的身体
好像战争中的达姆达姆鼓
他爱你
然而
你不知道想些什么

如果你曾经喜欢
在你的床尾
触碰他的手指
如果你曾经喜欢
对他说
那些不会流逝的话语
如果您曾经能够这样
为什么您还是离开了他呢?

Il faut apprendre
à se séparer
connaître les mécanismes
qui aident à s'éloigner
sans briser les liens
sans casser les sentiments
Il faut apprendre
à se quitter
sans se peredre

Retrouver
le temps à l'envers
les libertés
et les sommeils d'avant
Les heures m'étouffent
Les années me martèlent
Je n'en peux plus
de ces vagues déferlantes

La solitude
n'a pas de frontière
et elle est plus vieille que toi
si tu l'oublies parfois
elle te rattrape
à mi-chemin

Laisse-moi poser ma tête
sur le fleuve endormi
Ta force entraîne la mienne

必须学会分离
必须知道机械装置
会令彼此疏远
同时却不挣断绳索
不破坏感情
必须学会离开
同时却不迷失自己

重新发现
反面的时间
重新发现
自由和前面的睡眠
一小时一小时让我喘不过气
一年一年不断侵扰着我
我再也不能
承受如此汹涌的浪潮

孤独
没有边界
她比你更苍老
如果有时你忘记了她
她重新抓住你
在中途

让我将自己的头枕在沉睡的江河上吧
你的力量牵动我的力量
你的沉默回答我

Tes silences me réspondent
Donne-moi la main
tu sais si bien
qui je suis

给我手吧
你如此清楚
我是谁

（姜玢　译）

In the naming

Keorapetse Kgositsile

We now know past any argument
that places can have scars
and they can be warm
or cold or full of intrigue
like faces.
                    Since the settler
set his odious foot here in 1820,
my Caribbean brother might say,
these hills have not been joyful together

In Rhini you can go up
or down or any direction
in the lay of the land where
the people have memories as palpable
as anything you can see with your own eye

But in Grahamstown,
those who know say,
any where you go is uphill

在命名中

[南非] 凯奥拉佩策·考斯尔

超出任何辩论，我们如今知道
地方会有疤痕
它们会温暖
或寒冷或像面孔
充满诡计。
　　　　　　　自从1820年
殖民者可憎的脚踏到此处，
我的加勒比兄弟会说，
这些山就不曾一同快乐过

在利尼你可以
向任何方向走
在它的地形中
人们拥有的记忆鲜明如
你用自己的眼睛所能看见的任何事物

但在格雷厄姆斯敦①，
那些了解的人说，
你去任何地方都是上坡

（冷霜　译）

---

① 南非共和国东开普省主要城市，利尼是其郊区。译注。

Debris

Amanda Hammar

What is lost lies scattered like debris
in a desolate wasteland:

faded blue school dress, pockets
ink-stained, proud hem unravelled;
a teacher's worn briefcase gaping open,
spilling pens and promise on the ground;

sweat-stained hoe, splintered door,
fire-blackened pot, charred blanket,
plowshares draped in spiders' webs,
random fragments of glass, iron, clay, thatch;

flapping in the wind, yellowed news-sheet
shamed by its own print; beneath it
pressed into mud, a mosaic of dried blood
and bone in silent invocation;

and caught in the rusted barbs of a fence
folded in on itself, a flame tree's waxy
orange blossom still full with the memory
of its own magnificence.

残骸

［津巴布韦］阿曼达·哈玛

废弃的荒原
那些四散丢失的像残骸：

褪色蓝校服，口袋
都沾染墨迹，庆幸那些衣褶被拆开；
老师破损的公文袋撕开大口，
将钢笔和那些允诺洒落一地；

锄头布满汗迹，门裂成碎片
火熏黑的壶罐，烧焦的地毯
犁头被织上了蛛网，
到处是玻璃、铁器、陶瓷和屋顶草的碎片；

而那些黄色的新闻小报，在风中摇晃
为自己的报道而羞愧；它的背面
被压进泥土，像在沉默中祈祷的干枯的
血和骨头，被打上了马赛克；

目光中偶遇围栏生锈的尖刺
密密麻麻交织一起，一棵火树苍白
但那些橘色的花簇仍充满着
壮丽的回忆。

（张伟栋　译）

A Day Made of Songs

Obododimma Oha

Would you, wouldn't you, said the wren
To the breaking day
The last night's dew left few
With thoughts of flight
The very question on the lips of the flowers
Is how a sunny story wakes from the mirth
Of an open sky

Would you, wouldn't you drink the approaching afternoon
And kill a tribe with rhetoric
Wouldn't you chew your pen a little often
And spit out some stereotypes, stir the types
Of emotions between the twin gongs

Would you, wouldn't you termite
The varying labour & a uniform rhythm of response
Each aspiration that chases the delicate day
To its longest shadows
Some distant welcomes you have not known, may never know
As they whisper or whimper the surest good evening
To an imminent storm

歌唱日

[尼日利亚] 奥波多迪玛·奥哈

你愿不愿意，鹪鹩
对破晓说
当思想联翩
夜露变得稀疏
这样的问题正含在花唇中：
灿烂的故事怎么从长空的
欢乐中醒来？

你愿不愿意啜饮这来临的下午
灭绝部落用修辞
你不想稍微频繁地动用笔墨
唱出某些老调，唤起
两个响韵间的激情？

你愿不愿意像白蚁
那分工不同但又统一的反应节奏
渴望着追逐美好的一天
直到暮色来临
某些遥远的欢迎你不知道，可能从不知道
当它们嘀咕或呜咽着最美好的夜晚
向即将来临的风暴。

（余旸　译）

are you the river or am i

Shabbir Banoobhai

are you the river or am i
do i flow into the sea or do you flow into me
why is it when i try to slake my thirst you disappear
when you try, i appear

you have never stopped calling me
i have never stopped answering you
whose longing elicited this longing in me
whose love buried me in sorrow

i, even i, even as i am
know the loneliness of separation
as sails of clouds, like memories
flee across the windswept sky

you are all that i love, all that i can love
yet how do i love you, know you, know that i love you
when all that you are remains unknown to me
and all that i am is known only to you

i carry within me the grief of all loving
would you be different if i knew you
would i be different - can a flower know
what it means to be a flower

你或我谁是河流

[南非] 沙比尔·巴努海

你或我谁是河流
我流入大海还是你流入我
为何我想止渴你却消失
当你想止渴我便出现

你唤我不止
我应答不止
谁之热望诱出我之热望
谁之爱慕埋葬我于悲伤

我，即便我，即便如我
亦知隔绝造就之孑然
一如云朵浮掠，一如记忆
逃离长风拂乱的长空

你是我爱之全部，我爱所能及之全部
即便我对你一无所知
即便我仅为你所知
我仍爱你，知你，知我爱你

我承载爱之全部哀愁
若我知你，你可会不同
我可会不同——花朵可会知晓
身为花朵之含义

all the silt of my journeying
all the salt of my yearning flows into you
and all longing, every love, all knowing, every loss
everything you are comes to rest in me

我携来的全部泥沙
我流向你之思慕的全部盐分
全部慕与爱，全部知与失
你的一切皆来栖身于我

（韩博　译）

Parrot at Sea

Dorian Haarhoff

I wonder at wave edge
how to portray
this scape, this twilight,
its colour swell and rise.

a woman walks out of the mist.
her parrot claws
and crabs her shoulder
in a treasure of images.

the great feathered body
of an African grey
puffs in the breeze sea.
cherry tail streaks the sky.

it echoes, mimics
the shuffle of waves,
the creak of a boat,
in pirate genes and gems.

the scuffed waves of its neck
leads to a beak where shells
embed in sandwash.
the sun sets in its iris eye.

海洋鹦鹉

［南非/纳米比亚］多利安·哈尔霍夫

我疑惑海浪边缘
该如何描画
这图景，这薄暮
它的毛色凹凸竖起。

一个女人步出迷雾。
她的鹦鹉
在这幅珍贵的图像中
爪和铁钳挂上肩头。

这只非洲灰鹦鹉
硕大的羽毛身体
海风中，鼓胀呼啸。
樱红的尾巴涂抹，使天空布满条纹。

以海盗的基因和宝石
它鸣响，模仿着
海浪的浑浊
和船舰的裂帛声。

她脖子处划伤的羽毛纹理中
伸出一个像贝壳
嵌入沙堆积中的鸟嘴
太阳落于它的眼瞳。

（叶美　译）

Lake Haven

Joyce Chigiya

On the right side of level headed Haven hill
beside the largest body of water inland
that sits eyeing the heavens, going up to the feet
of musasa trees, up to the neck of the water hyacinth
is Lake Haven.

On a windy day the turquoise water is hushed
as it is tossed in harsh waves; sh-sh-sh-sh-sh
for it will be caught on the haven shore
and lulled to sleep on the water-bed.

The sweet-toothed monkeys trip with their tails
(in the hesitant moment of which to put first, tail or paw)
sugar basins set in the shades outdoors, on concrete tables
for brunches, to swing up branches with morsels of the diamante granules.

At dusk, siesta is over for the hippopotamus
scattering the water fowl as they come out to go feeding
their spacious backs, patches on the water
like stepping stones all the way up to the haven.

When the Libra moon splashes onto the lake
illuminating the boatsmen out for a catch

海文湖①

[津巴布韦] 乔伊斯·齐基娅

就在平顶的海文山右侧
最大的内陆水域之畔，上升到
姆萨沙树脚下，与水葫芦的脖子
齐平的，就是海文湖
它凝视着天穹

在风中，宝石绿的湖水随着波浪
静静翻滚：嘘——嘘——嘘——嘘
水会在岸边被接纳
又沉沉睡入湖底

馋嘴的猴子摇尾潜行
（爪子和尾巴，哪个在先，它们一刻犹豫）
户外的阴影里，早餐的糖盆
就摆在水泥桌上，甜蜜的颗粒晶莹挂满

黄昏，河马午休完毕
外出觅食，惊起四方水禽
它们后脊开阔，浮游于水上
像是踏脚的石块，一路通向海文

当天秤之月照耀湖面
诱使船夫外出渔猎

---

① Lake Haven，Haven有避难所之意，诗中的musasa trees除指植物名称，还有临时居所之意。译注。

a thousand lights gyrate with vigour in the water
like mass display girls doing the kwasa-kwasa.

The lion's ramble from across, rattles the chalet's windows
like an earth tremour, the peacock, having set his dish
makes a wake up call to his various 'only' loves
as eighteen-wheeler trucks groan across the bridge, Masvingo bound.

The moans of bacon lying on the grill and the smell it emits,
the lavender floor polish waft through the kitchen window
to be dammed in the coolness caught between the underground lake
and the flora ceiling, sending out invitations to breakfast.

月光飘洒水上，如一群女孩
跳着哇塞－哇塞舞①

漫游的狮子，咆哮声像大地震颤
小屋的窗子也嘎嘎作响，而孔雀，摆好了菜肴
给他的各位相好电话叫早，当十八轮的卡车
低吼过桥，那里就是马旬戈②的边界。

培根在烤架上滋滋作响，肉味弥漫
地板闪闪发亮，也隔了厨房窗子散出草香
在地下湖和葱茏草木之间
又有凉爽沁入，发出一份早餐的邀请。

（姜涛　译）

---

① 来自刚果的一种舞蹈。译注。
② 津巴布韦的一个省。译注。

Good Morning

Joyce Chigiya

The hills are sitting in the east, the focal point
dark looming forms hump-backing the land sky high
border the dim stage below where birds perform
"The cook of the roost in the sky is nigh"

Silver plate in the west, its day done
takes a leap for the wings with a moon walker's
immunity to gravity, to make way, secret lover-style
Cuckoldoodle-doo! Venus closes her eyes
at the approach of the Man

popping up, sweet as a Mazoe orange
sprinkling sherbet onto the plains of Chivhu
the dew ridding on the grass, sparkles
like a welcome bride newly eloped.

早安

[津巴布韦] 乔伊斯·齐基娅

群山坐落东方，天地之间
黑暗迫近，隆起如驼峰
在广大深暗之下，鸟儿出演：
"空中禽鸟合炊就要来临"

银盘在西，已成的日子
像登月者摆脱重力，展翅轻跃
向前，隐秘地示爱
咕咕啼①！维纳斯合上双目
当着一个男人临近

迸发吧！像马佐韦②的橘子一样清甜
把汁液洒向奇武③平原
露珠从草上滑落，耀眼迷人
如一位刚刚落跑的新娘。

(姜涛 译)

---

① 公鸡打鸣声。译注。
② 津巴布韦的一条小溪。译注。
③ 津巴布韦的一个小镇。译注。

Mutserendende
—from Sliding game

Chirikuré Chirikuré

Every little boy in my village
Can describe with joy and pride
How you play the mutserendende game.
You chop a healthy munhanzva tree
Cut the branches off the stem
Then drag the log up a mountain

Like Jesus Christ on a donkey
You mount the log, holding tight
Then, woosh, you zoom down

It's so fast and furious
Eyes closed, breath held
You surrender all to fate

You land with a big thud
Your backsides tattered
Bleeding in hot ecstasy

So do many among us
Leading life fast and furious
Landing with tattered, bleeding souls

姆瑟轮丹①
——节选自《滑树游戏》

[津巴布韦] 齐里克热·齐里克热

我村里的每一个小男孩
都能够眉飞色舞地描绘
你怎么来玩姆瑟轮丹
你砍一棵健壮的穆含瓦树
把枝条从树干上砍下
然后拉着原木上山

就像耶稣骑在毛驴上
你跨着原木，死死抱紧
然后，嗖，你直落而下

如此快而猛烈
眼睛紧闭，呼吸屏住
完全降服于命运

呼地一声巨响你落地了
你的屁股摔烂
流着血却狂热销魂

我们中间好多人也是如此
生命行驶得快而猛烈
停下时灵魂头破血流

（成婴　译）

---

① 本诗是《滑树游戏》的一部分，作者强调此诗主要写砍伐树木，对环境不友善以及游戏中的人的冒险天性。译注。

In the void

Hama Tuma

I hear music in the wind
the tam tam of festive drums
        riding the clouds
I see the dawn of joy
        in the tears of a hungry child
Touch love as it flies past
        Horse-riding a bullet
I hear music in the void
the trees are still, unmoving
and no heart beat is heard.
I dance to the tune of death,
desolate. I am all alone
in the desert.

在虚空中

[埃塞俄比亚] 哈玛·图玛

我听着风中的音乐
咚咚的欢庆鼓声
　　　　乘着云朵
我看见欢乐的黎明
　　　　在饥饿孩子的泪水中
触到了爱，当它飞过
　　　　骑着一颗子弹
我听着虚空中的音乐
树木静默，不动
也听不到心的跳动。
我随着死亡的曲调起舞，
孤独地。我独自一人
在沙漠中。

（张曙光　译）

Origins of the Dance

Nii Ayikwei Parkes

Talkative though the drum
might be it knows how to

start a beat
root a movement

in the sweet diggings
it conjures. But late arrivals

to the dance can never quite
fall in step unless they can find

the beginning of the poly-
rhythm; something the ancestors buried

along with our sense of self.
Might be why when we reach loose ends

we begin to excavate, reach back
like starved, scattered Sankofa birds

for the primal egg of ourselves, the knot
I felt in my stomach the first time

I clasped the curve of the jembe between

舞之源

[加纳] 奈伊·阿伊克维·帕克斯

鼓虽饶舌
也许因为它知道

如何一击
在接连掘进中

植入一个动作
但迟到的舞者

不会安静地潜入
除非他们能找到

那杂沓节奏的开端
那先人埋下的

一直伴随了"我觉"。
这便是为什么,渐进尾声

我们就开始穿凿、回溯
像饥饿的失群小鸟

寻找自我最初的卵,那个结儿
我第一次感觉在胃中

我扣紧两腿间手鼓的曲线

my thighs, extracted the first deep throb

of heart music under the watchful eye
of the wind and our Form Three tutor

and understood that it didn't matter
whether the bird, egg, dance or beat

came first, as long as when they emerge
they are intertwined, tied at the core.

在风的注视下

在第三教练的注视下
释放心乐第一次深深的震颤。

我明了，无论
鸟、卵、舞、鼓

不分先后，只要出现
就互为彼此，内部连成一体

（姜涛　译）

Chi Kung

Dorian Haarhoff

you stand grounded,
loose-legged.
scenes of Chinese parks
and a thousand pictograms
rise in your eyes.
we sway, trees in a breeze
to find the centre force
in taproot, bark, sap and branch.
arm flap like prayer flags,
wrapping us in wind.
we slap slack-limbed the body
to wake the cells
from misty sleep.
taps kidneys to chi them.
stretch toes and arch backs.
then we raise and drop arms,
a child on a swing , higher, wilder
above the hills at this retreat
down to the fulcrum forest of knees.
we elongate foot to root
to hot rock, fingers to tree top
to eagle's path, Buddha sky.
we soar with you, winged beings,
landing lightly on trees.
pull the elasticity of the world

济公

[南非/纳米比亚] 多利安·哈尔霍夫

你双脚落地时，
轻松地站住。
眼底升起
中国园林美景
和一千个象形文字。
我们身体摆动，像微风的树
寻找树根，树皮，树液，树枝的
力心。
轻拍手臂似令旗
风中包裹我们。
我们掌击这呆滞四肢
唤醒躯体内部
迷朦嗜睡的细胞。
我们拍动肾脏吃它们。
活动脚趾，弓起背。
然后抬高，平落双臂，
像荡秋千的孩童，升高，狂野
在山岗隐居地
一直下降到膝盖的森林支点。
我们伸长双脚至地心
触到了热岩石，十指碰到树杪
碰到鹰的路，佛陀的天空。
我们跟随你飞翔，展翼的造物，
轻轻地降落树间。
在食指和拇指之间

between fore and thumb.
we slip back to earth.
become the sunflower at rest
rising to follow the gold
folding to greet the light.
the force new formed flows
along meridians and love lines
beneath our fingers.
skin flower fresh
we belong to this now day.

赢得这个弹性的世界
悄声返回地面。
我们变成了静息的向日葵
随金色的阳光升起
又弯身问候。
十指间
新生命力沿
经脉和爱情线流淌。
皮肤开出鲜嫩的花
我们属于此刻的今天。

（叶美　译）

Night

Wole Soyinka

Your hand is heavy. Night, upon my brow,
I bear no heart mercuric like the clouds, to dare
Exacerbation from your subtle plough.

Woman as a clam, on the sea's cresent
I saw your jealous eye quench the sea's
Fluorescence, dance on the pulse incessant

Of the waves. And I stood, drained
Submitting like the sand, blood and brine
Coursing to the roots. Night, you rained

Serrated shadows through dank leaves
Till, bathed in warm suffusion of your dappled cells
Sensations pained me, faceless, silent as night thieves.

Hide me now, when night children haunt the earth
I must hear none! These misted calls will yet
Undo me; naked, unbidden, at Night's muted birth.

夜

[尼日利亚] 沃莱·索因卡

你的手很重。夜，压在我的眉棱上。
我身上没有飘忽不定的水银心，不敢
因为你莫测的行进情绪激动。

女人如蚌，在海上的新月中
我看到你妒嫉的眼睛熄灭了
海的荧光，随着波浪的脉搏

不停地跳舞。而我站着，干枯，
卑顺，如沙子，血和盐水
奔向树根。夜，你藉由阴冷的树叶

降下锯齿状影子
直到，充满你多斑的细胞的温暖又把我浸润
这感觉让我痛苦，无以名状，像夜里的贼一样静。

现在藏起我吧，当夜的孩子出没于大地
我一定听不到任何人！而这隐隐的召唤
也将让我释然，坦荡，情愿，在夜静静诞生之际。

（席亚兵　译）

II   Identity, History and Language

Oral tradition places poets at the centre of social life as storytellers, repositories of history, guardians of language, those charged with observing human values and commenting on the powerful. In this section poets lament the departed and advise the living, poems that describe the sacred act of communication, that links the human to God through the rhythmic cadences of emotional truth. Each individual speaks for a collective. Language and music are primal tools in creating the ritual of poetry, where we stand, naked before God and each other.

II 身份、历史与语言

在非洲的口述传统里，诗人被赋予社会生活的
说书人、历史的记录人与语言的保护人等多重角
色；他们以社会为己任，观察人生价值与评论当权
者。在这一章节里，诗人一边慨叹逝者，一边提醒
生者；诗歌成为交流的神圣工具，通过优美的韵律
与真挚的情感把人类与上天连为一体。每一位诗人
成为自己的族裔的代言人。语言与音乐是创造诗歌
仪式的根本工具；在仪式中，我们赤裸于上帝之前
和彼此之间。

Blewuu

Kofi Anyidoho

Blewuu... Blewuu... Akofa   Blewuuu...

Words are birds: They fly so fast   too far
for the hunter's aim.   Words are winds.
Sometimes they breeze gentle upon the smiles
our hearts may wear for joy.   They fan the sweat
away from fever's brow.   They lull our minds
to sleep upon the soft breast of Earth.
Yet soon   too soon   words become the mad dreams
of storms: They howl through caves   through joys
into shrines of thunderbolts.   They leave a ghost
on guard at memory's door.   Therefore
gently ... gently ... Akofa, ge-nt-ly...
take care what images of life
your tongue may carve for show
at carnivals of weary souls.

慢慢地

[加纳] 科菲·阿尼多赫

慢些……慢些……阿科法　慢慢地……

词语是鸟儿：　作为猎人的目标
它们飞得太快　太远。　词语是风。
有时他们温柔地吹上微笑
我们的心会因喜悦而疲惫。　它们从发热的额头
吹去汗水。　　它们哄着我们的心智
在大地柔软的胸膛上入睡。
然而快了　太快了　词语变成风暴
疯狂的梦：　它们吼叫着穿过洞穴　穿过喜悦
进入闪亮的雷电。　　它们留下一个幽灵
守护着记忆的门。　　因此
慢些……慢些……阿科法，慢慢地……
当心那些生命的形象
你的舌头会被切下
在疲惫灵魂的狂欢中展出。

（张曙光　译）

Knobkerrie

Chirikuré Chirikuré

We undertook this long journey
You, leading the way in this jungle
Wielding that ancestral knobkerrie
Passed on to us by our departed sekuru

With ernomous pride and gentle dignity
You cleared lions and jackals off the path
And clobbered game for us to feast enroute
As we covered mile after mile with ease
We went over mountains and valleys with ease
Until you wielded the knobkerrie against me
In a heated quarrel over which direction to take
And the heritage slipped, falling down the cliff

Does it really matter now
Whether to go left or right
When jackals are licking the knobkerrie
As it lies forlorn in the valley, head down?

圆头棒

[津巴布韦] 齐里克热·齐里克热

我们承受着漫长的旅途
你，在丛林中为我们开路
挥舞着祖先的圆头棒
他传自我们已逝的祖父

无比荣耀，显赫尊贵
你清除路途中的狮子和黑背豺
这技艺绝活是为了让我们飨宴途中
我们轻松走过一哩又一哩
轻松走过高山和峡谷
直到你挥舞着圆头棒朝我而来
因为我们为要走哪个方向而激烈争吵
传家宝滑落，坠下山崖

往左还是往右
现在真的重要吗
当豺狼啃着圆头棒
当它头朝下，孤零零地躺进山谷？

（成婴　译）

71

In the Balance

Dorian Haarhoff

this woman loops sticks
in a ring of wire,
bundled into one load.
she steps out of the desert
bearing wood for one fire.

this pile will flicker away
part of the night in a
dry quick burn. this snap
of kindling raised
on head and arms.

she moves as one
on high wire, the pole
extending outstretched arms
to hold the see-saw centre
sprung across shoulders.

above the hushed ancestor crowd
who will her not to fall
off the dust-line into hunger,
she balances for a moment
her family in these branches.

配置

[南非/纳米比亚] 多利安·哈尔霍夫

这个女人
把散乱的木柴，
整齐地围着一束。
她抱起生火的木料
快步走出这荒漠之地。

它们将是一场干燥快速地
燃烧，在夜晚的角落
远远地闪烁。点火的劈啪声
迅速串入头和手臂。

她移走像一个人
踩钢丝，横出两侧的木头
是延伸扩展的手臂
越过肩膀
支撑住了这跷跷板的身体。

天上众多祖先
安静地希望她不要
被灰尘线绊住，跌入饥饿，
一分钟后她在这些树枝上
为家人配置食物。

（叶美　译）

The Departed
—for a friend, deceased

Stanley Onjezani Kenani

your smile is still alive in our hearts
your sense of humour, your laughter

the jokes are still fresh in our minds
the inexplicable kindness, the indescribable greatness,

your face still shines at us in our dreams
your big white teeth, your charming dimples,

the sweet songs you sang still ring in our ears
the rich deep voice, the melancholy dirges,

your voice still plays in our moments of solitude
your fireside stories, your profound wisdom,

the last words you said to Mama have been chronicled
the emptiness in us, the meaninglessness of life.

死者
——给一位逝去的朋友

[马拉维] 斯坦利·昂热扎尼·克那尼

你的笑仍在我们心里活着
你的幽默感，笑声

那些玩笑仍在我们脑中生机如故
那些难以言表的仁慈，无可描述的崇高，

你的脸仍在我们的梦中闪耀
你整齐而白的牙齿，迷人的酒窝

你唱过的甜蜜歌曲仍在我们的耳中回旋
那浑厚的声音，忧伤的挽歌，

我们独处的时候你的嗓音仍在演奏
你那些炉边故事和你的无尽智慧，

你对妈妈的最后的话被编入
我们的虚无和无意义的生命。

（张伟栋　译）

Still born

Tjawangwa Dema

How did you know to run
To enter this world through a back door
Leave before you have come
Across colour and grass
And all the things in between

Then and now

How did you know to run
Fast enough not to feel
The first of many winds
Catching only the shadow of your back
A breath held but never taken

仍旧诞生①

［博茨瓦纳］贾旺娃·迪玛

你怎么知道通过一道后门
跑着进入这世界
在你来到之前离开
穿过颜色和草地
以及中间的一切

那时和现在

你怎么知道要跑得足够快
以致感觉不到
诸多风中的第一阵
抓到的只是你的背影
一个呼吸保住了但永远不进行

（周伟驰　译）

---

① 这首诗是写一个死婴的诞生的。译注。

Sorting

Makhosazana Xaba

He approaches; a coffee mug in his hands
and a smile on his face. He puts it on the bedside table
then, he bends over to help me sort out
the varied miniature containers holding:
folding toothbrushes of many colours,
single-use toothpaste tubes,
ear muffs, eye covers, hand cream,
miniature pens, notebooks, pairs of socks,
moisturisers and a selection of haberdashery.

We put things in groups
and throw away empty containers.
We count the groups and the items in each group
and place them in order on his bed.
This is taking a lot of time.
We smile wordlessly, knowing
the question in both our heads:
how can one accumulate so many
of these miniature things
that they need so much sorting?
The same smile is on my face
when I open my eyes and realize
it's the twenty third day after his death.

整理

[南非] 马克霍萨萨纳·萨巴

他靠近；一个大咖啡杯攥在手心
脸挂着笑。他把它放上床头柜
然后，弯身帮我整理
这个装满各种微小物件的货箱：
五彩的折叠牙刷，
单人牙膏
耳套，眼罩，手霜，
小钢笔，笔记本，几搭短袜，
润肤霜和几款男装。

我将它们堆放一起
扔掉了空货箱。
我们数好后，贴上条目
按顺序摆在他的床上。
这花掉了一些时间。
我们脸上挂满无言的笑，心
生出一个问题：
一个人怎么积攒下这么多
小物件
以至花这么多力气整理它们？
那笑此刻也出现在我脸上，
当我睁开眼，认识到
这是他死后的第二十三天。

（叶美　译）

Shilling Love

Shailja Patel

One

They never said / they loved us

Those words were not / in any language / spoken by my parents

I love you honey was the dribbled caramel / of Hollywood movies / Dallas / Dynasty / where hot water gushed / at the touch of gleaming taps / electricity surged / 24 hours a day / through skyscrapers banquets obscene as the Pentagon / were mere backdrops / where emotions had no consequences words / cost nothing meant nothing would never have to be redeemed

My parents / didn't speak / that / language

1975 / 15 Kenyan shillings to the British pound / my mother speaks battle

Storms the bastions of Nairobi's / most exclusive prep schools / shoots our cowering / six-year old bodies like cannonballs / into the all-white classrooms / scales the ramparts of class distinction / around Loreto convent / where the president / sends his daughter / the government ministers, foreign diplomats / send their daughters / because my mother's daughters / will / have world-class educations

She falls / regroups / falls and re-groups / in endless assaults on visa

先令之爱

[肯尼亚] 莎尔遮·佩特尔

一

他们从不说 / 他们爱我们

那些字眼不属于 / 我父母所说的 / 任何一种语言

《我爱你宝贝》是好莱坞电影 / 垂涎欲滴的黄油奶糖 / 《达拉斯》/《王朝》/ 那里热水喷流 / 只要一碰那闪亮的龙头 / 感情奔涌 / 一天24小时 / 在摩天大楼的盛宴中下流的五角大楼 / 只不过是布景 / 那里感情没有任何结果言语 / 没有任何付出没有任何意义也没有任何必须的救赎

我的父母 / 不说 / 那种 / 语言

1975年 /15肯尼亚先令兑一英镑 / 我妈妈说战斗

内罗毕最好的私立小学 / 顽固的轰鸣声 / 扑向我们畏缩的 / 六岁的身体像炮弹 / 落入全白色的教室里 / 把班级里差别的壁垒升高成 / 雷洛托修道院的围墙 / 总统把女儿 / 送入这里 / 政府部长，外国外交官 / 也把女儿送来 / 因为我妈妈的女儿 / 要受 / 世界一流的教育

她失败了 / 重振旗鼓 / 失败了又重振旗鼓 / 不屈不挠

officials / who sneer behind their bulletproof windows / at US and British consulates / my mother the general / arms her daughters / to take on every citadel

1977 / 20 Kenyan shillings to the British pound / my father speaks / stoic endurance he began at 16 the brutal apprenticeship / of a man who takes care of his own / relinquished dreams of / fighter pilot rally driver for the daily crucifixion / of wringing profit from a small business / my father the foot soldier, bound to an honour / deeper than any currency / *you must* / *finish what you start you must* / *march until you drop you must* / *give your life for those* / *you bring into the world*

I try to explain love / in shillings / to those who've never gauged / who gets to leave who has to stay / who breaks free and what they pay / those who've never measured love / by every rung of the ladder / from survival / to choice

A force as grim and determined / as a boot up the backside / a spur that draws blood a mountaineer's rope / that yanks / relentlessly / up

My parents never say / they love us / they save and count / count and save / the shilling falls against the pound / college fees for overseas students / rise like flood tides / love is a luxury / priced in hard currency / ringed by tariffs / and we devour prospectuses / of ivied buildings smooth lawns vast / libraries the way Jehovah's witnesses / gobble visions of paradise / because we know we'll have to be / twice as good three times as fast four times as driven / with angels powers and principalities on our side just / to get / on / the / plane

地向签证官攻击／他们在防弹窗后面讥笑／在美国和英国领事馆／我的将军妈妈／武装她的女儿／攻下每一座堡垒

1977年／20肯尼亚先令兑一英镑／我的父亲说／顺从天意的他16岁就开始残酷的学徒期／学做一个自立的男人／放弃当战斗机飞行员公路赛车手的／梦想钉死在每天挣钱的十字架上／从微末的事业中挤压出一点利润／我的步兵父亲，执着于一种荣誉／比任何货币更深／*你必须／完成你开始做的事情你必须／向前直到你倒下你必须／把你的生命献给那些／你带入这个世界的人*

我试图解释爱／先令里的爱／向那些从未掂量过／谁离开谁必须留下／谁获得自由和要付出什么的人／向那些从未计量过／通过在生存的梯子上／每上一级／的选择来计量爱的人

一种残酷坚定的力量／像踹在屁股上的一脚／溅出血的一刺像登山者的绳索／猛拽／不停地／向上

我的父母从不说／他们爱我们／他们存钱和数钱／数钱和存钱／肯尼亚先令对英镑的汇率下跌／留学生的大学学费／洪水般上涨／爱是一种奢侈／用硬通货计价／被关税紧绕／我们吞食着招生简章／爬满常春藤的楼平整的草坪巨大的／图书馆如上帝的见证／吞咽着天堂的奇观／因为我们知道我们只得是／双倍的好三倍的快四倍的努力靠天使之力 和公国的眷顾我们恰好／登／上了／那架／飞机

Thirty shillings to the pound forty / shillings to the pound / my parents fight over money late in the night / my father pounds the walls and yells / *I can't –it's impossible – what do you think I am?* / My mother propels us through school tuition exams applications / locks us into rooms to study / keeps an iron grip on the bank books

1982 / gunshots / in the streets of Nairobi / military coup leaders / thunder over the radio / Asian businesses wrecked and looted Asian women raped / after / the government / regains control / we whisper what the coup leaders planned

Round up all the Asians at gunpoint / in the national stadium / strip them of whatever / they carry / march them 30 miles / elders in wheelchairs / babies in arms / march them 30 miles to the airport / pack them onto any planes / of any foreign airline / tell the pilots / down the rifle barrels / *leave* / *we don't care where you take them* / *leave*

I learn like a stone in my gut that / third-generation Asian Kenyan will never / be Kenyan enough / all my patriotic fervor / will never turn my skin black / as yet another western country / drops a portcullis / of immigration spikes / my mother straps my shoulders back with a belt / to teach me / to stand up straight

50 Kenyan shillings to the pound / we cry from meltdown pressure / of exam after exam where second place is never good enough / they snap / faces taut with fear / *you can't be soft* / *you have to fight* / *or the world will eat you up*

三十先令兑一英镑四十/先令兑一英镑/我的父母为钱战斗到深夜/我的父亲击打着墙叫喊/*我不能——这不可能——你以为我是什么？*/我妈妈驱动着我们通过学费考试申请/把我们锁在屋子里学习/铁腕抓着银行存折

1982年/枪声/在内罗毕的街上响起/军事政变的领袖们/在收音机里雷鸣般叫喊/亚裔的生意被砸被抢亚裔妇女被强奸/后来/政府/恢复了控制/我们咬耳朵说政变领袖们计划过

集合起所有亚裔用枪口对着/在国家体育馆/剥夺他们/所带的一切/让他们行走30英里/老人坐在轮椅上/婴儿抱在怀里/让他们行军30英里到机场/把他们塞进任何一架飞机/任何一条国外的航线/告诉飞行员/把枪管放低/*飞走吧/我们不管你把他们运到哪里去/飞走吧*

像有一块石头在身体里我认识到/三代的亚裔肯尼亚人将永远/不足以成为肯尼亚人/我所有的爱国狂热/永远不会把我的皮肤变黑/随着另一个西方国家/拉下带刺的/移民的铁闸门/我妈妈用一条背带把我的肩膀向后勒紧/教育我/要站得挺直

50肯尼亚先令兑一英镑/我们在过度的压力下叫喊/这一个接一个的考试获第二名就是失败/他们控制不住/脸皮被怕变厚/*你们不能软弱/你们只好攻击/或者这世界会好好吃你*

75 Kenyan shillings to the pound / they hug us / tearless stoic at airports / as we board planes for icy alien England / cram instructions into our pockets like talismans / *Eat proper meals so you don't get sick / cover your ears against the cold / avoid those muffathias / the students without purpose or values / learn and study / succeed / learn and study / succeed / remember remember remember the cost of your life*

they never say / they love us

Two

I watch how I love / I admonish exhort / like a Himalayan guide I / rope my chosen ones / yank them remorselessly up / when they don't even want to be / on the frigging mountain

like a vigilante squad I / scan dark streets for threats I / strategize for war and famine I / slide steel down spines

I watch heat steam off my skin / when Westerners drop *I love you's* into conversation / like blueberries hitting / soft / muffin dough / I convert it to shillings / and I wince

December 2000 / 120 shillings to the British pound / 90 Kenyan shillings to the US dollar / my sister Sneha and I / wait for our parents / at San Francisco's international terminal

75肯尼亚先令兑一英镑/他们抱住我们/坚决无泪在机场/当我们要登机飞往冰冷陌生的英国/往我们的口袋里塞各种指南就像塞护身符/*多吃点儿肉这样你们就不会生病/戴上耳套防冻/避开那些放荡的女孩/那些没有目标或价值的同学/好好学习认真思考/获得成功/好好学习认真思考/获得成功/记住记住记住你们生活的付出*

他们从不说/他们爱我们

二

我观赏我爱的程度/我警告劝诫/像一个喜马拉雅山的登山向导我/用绳子拉着我选定的人/不加考虑地猛拽着他们/向上/甚至在他们根本就不想去到那/该死的山上时

像一个自愿的巡逻队员/我搜查黑街潜伏的威胁/我备战备荒我/悄悄给脊柱加上钢条

我看着热气从我的皮肤蒸腾/当西方人滴答/*我爱你*到了闲扯/像蓝莓很诱人/柔软的/松饼面团/我把它换算成先令/我畏缩地退出

2000年12月/120肯尼亚先令兑一英镑/90先令兑一美元/我的妹妹斯内哈和我/等着我们的父母/在旧金山国际候机楼

Four hours after / their plane landed / they have not emerged

And we know with the hopeless rage / of third-world citizens /
African passport holders / that the sum of their lives and labour /
dreams and sacrifice / was measured sifted weighed found / want-
ing / by the INS

Somewhere deep in the airport's underbelly / in a room rank with
fear and despair / my parents / who have travelled / 27 hours /
across three continents / to see their children / are interrogated / by
immigration officials

My father the footsoldier / numb with exhaustion / is throwing
away / all the years / with reckless resolve / telling them / *take the
passports / take them / stamp them / no readmission EVER / just let me
out to see my daughters*

My mother the general / dizzy with desperation / cuts him off
shouts him down / demands *listen to me I'm the one / who filled in
the visa forms / in her mind her lip curls*
she thinks / *these Americans / call themselves so advanced so / mod-
ern but still / in the year 2000 / they think it must be the husband in
charge / they won't let the wife speak*

On her face a lifetime / of battle-honed skill and charm / turns
like a heat lamp / onto the INS man until he / stretches / yawns /
relents / he's tired / it's late / he wants his dinner / and my parents
/ trained from birth / to offer Indian / hospitality / open their bags
and give their sandwiches / to this man / who would have sent

他们的飞机落地 / 四个小时之后 / 他们还没出现

我们怀着无奈的愤怒得知 / 作为第三世界公民 / 非洲
护照持有人 / 他们的生活和劳作 / 梦想和风险 / 需要 /
由移民归化局 / 来测定筛选过秤找到

在机场地下很深的某处 / 在一个充满恐惧和绝望的
房间 / 我的父母 / 他们奔波了 / 27小时 / 穿越了三块
大陆 / 来看他们的孩子 / 移民局的官员 / 在盘问他们

我的步兵父亲 / 因精疲力竭而木然 / 丢掉了 / 这么多
年的谨慎忍耐 / 不顾一切地 / 对他们说 / *拿走护照吧* /
拿走吧 / *给它们戳章* / *无需再次入境的许可* / *只要让*
我出去见我的女儿

我的将军母亲 / 绝望得差点晕了 / 打断他的话叫他住
口 / 要求听我说我是 / *填签证表的人* / *想象中她的嘴*
唇在扭曲
她想着 / *这些美国人* / *自称那么进步那么* / *现代但仍*
以为 / *在2000年* / *还必须是丈夫掌管一切* / *他们不让*
妻子说话

在她的脸上那种终身 / 战斗所磨练的技能和魅力 / 变
成了一盏热灯 / 照着移民局的官员直到他 / 伸懒腰 /
打呵欠 / 终于发慈悲 / 他累了 / 时间很晚了 / 他要去
吃饭了 / 而我的父母 / 从出生就被教育 / 保持印度人
的乐善好施 / 打开他们的行李把他们的三明治递给 /

them back / without a thought

Sneha and I / in the darkened lobby / watch the empty exit
way / our whole American / dream-bought-with-their-lives
/ hisses mockery around our rigid bodies / we swallow sobs
because / they raised us to be tough / they raised us to be
fighters and into that / clenched haze / of not / crying

here they come

hunched / over their luggage carts our tiny / fierce / fragile /
dogged / indomitable parents

Hugged tight they stink / of 31 hours in transit / hugged
tighter we all stink / with the bravado of all the years / pain
bitten down on gargantuan hopes / holding on through
near-disasters / never ever / giving in / to softness

The stench rises off us / unbearable / of what / was never
said

Something / is bursting the walls of my arteries something
/ is pounding it's way up my throat like a volcano / rising /
finally / I understand / why I'm a poet

Because I was born to a law / that states / before you claim a
word you steep it / in terror and shit / in hope and joy and
grief / in labor endurance vision costed out / in decades of

这个人 / 他本来要把他们送回去 / 想都不想一下

斯内哈和我 / 在暗下来的大堂里 / 看着空荡荡的出口 /
我们整个的美国 / 梦 – 买下 – 用 – 他们的 – 生计 / 他们
一生都携带着它 / 在我们僵硬的身体四周发出嗤嗤
的冷笑 / 我们吞咽着暗泣因为 / 他们培育我们做坚强
的人 / 他们培育我们成为斗士在那样 / 气愤的情境下
/ 不要 / 哭泣

他们出来了

弓着背 / 推着他们的行李车我们瘦小的 / 勇猛的 / 脆
弱的 / 顽强的 / 不屈不挠的父母

紧紧的拥抱他们经历了恶劣的 / 31 个小时的飞行过
境 / 更紧的拥抱我们全家人 / 凭着勇气度过了所有岁
月里的恶日子 / 痛苦啃啮着巨大的希望 / 在困境之中
坚持 / 永远不 / 屈服 / 陷入软弱

那种不愉快的感觉从我们身上升起 / 难以忍受 / 这些 /
从未说出的难受

某种东西 / 要让我的血管爆裂某种东西 / 冲撞着涌上
我的喉咙像岩浆 / 涌起 / 最后 / 我明白了 / 为什么我
是一个诗人

因为我为这部法律而生 / 它声明 / 在你赢得一个词之
前你沉浸于它 / 在恐惧和粪堆中 / 在希望和欢乐和悲
伤中 / 在劳动的忍耐的奇观中 / 在你生命数十年的耗

your life / you have to sweat and curse it / pray and keen
it / crawl and bleed it / with the very marrow / of your
bones / you have to earn / its / meaning

费中／你只好流汗并诅咒它／祈祷并渴求它／下跪并且流血／只好用尽你骨头里的／每一滴骨髓／去挣得／它的／意义

（雷武铃　译）

显像2　胡项城

（Appearance II　Hu Xiangcheng）

Poetry

Tolu Ogunlesi

Long before the conscious
Touch of cold whiteness
On black skin,
It snowed
In my mind

Poetry fell
from a dark sky
And froze my foolishness
Through its thin anorak

Metaphors watched over memories
Near the vacant fireplace;
Sgt. Poetry
Administering the Prison of Words

And a cold light polished
My words
To that fiendish glint
That startled God
And left my nameprint everywhere.

诗

[尼日利亚] 陶鲁·欧冈勒斯

在冷冷的白
有意碰到黑皮肤
之前很久，
我的脑子里
已经下雪了。

诗从黑暗的
天空落下，
并透过它的薄连帽衫
冻僵我的愚蠢。

隐喻在空壁炉边
监护记忆；
诗长官
掌管词语的监狱。

而一束冷光
擦亮我的词，
有关恶魔般闪光的词，
它震惊了上帝，
将我的名字印得到处都是。

（丁丽英　译）

when the first slave was brought to the cape

Shabbir Banoobhai

when the first slave was brought to the cape
he looked at the awesome mountain
which roots us to an eternal beauty
hundreds of years later, and affirmed

i am as free and as tall as this mountain
this mountain is more chained than i am
i will climb to the top one day
and call the adhaan before dawn

my voice will carry across the seas
to my loved ones in a land
i may never see again
and they will know that i

and the treasures i carry within me
are safe and always will be
for as long as beauty
and this mountain survive

当第一个奴隶被带到好望角

［南非］沙比尔·巴努海

当第一个奴隶被带到好望角
他凝视数百年后
仍带我们扎根恒久之美
那令人敬畏的山脉，断言

我与此山同等高峻且自由
此山所受束缚亦多于我
终有一日我将登顶
且于破晓之前呼吁祷告

我的声音将穿越海洋
去往我爱的一处陆地
我再也看不到它
但他们必将获悉

我及我心中的珍宝
尚且安好，将与
山脉之美
一并永存

（韩博 译）

Totems

Ama Ata Aidoo

I
Came upon an owl
at the crossroads
blinking with confusion
greater than
mine!

Bird of doom.
Bird of promise.

Fluorescent lightning on a
city corn-field,
tell the owl of
the changing times.

They-of-the-Crow
cannot
carve out
destinies through
marriage.

Whoever can?
He does
too well by her,

                                        and

图腾

[加纳] 阿玛·阿塔·艾杜

我
在叉道上
遇到一只猫头鹰
迷茫地眨着眼
比我还
严重!

末日之鸟
希望之鸟

城市的五光十色
闪耀在玉米地
告诉猫头鹰
时代变了

那——帮——乌——鸦
没法
用婚姻
改写
命运

谁又能?
他这般心满意足
和她在一起

　　　　　　　　　　　　而

she always
knows when
starched rags go to swaddle
another's baby.

Dodua of the light palms:
She is hanging out the
last new to dry from its
first washing.

Perch where you can, and
tell your story. They make
you believe that all roofs
cover homes from the rain.

Akua my sister,
No one chooses to stand
under a tree in a storm.

So
You
shall not be the one to remind
Me
to keen for the great ancesters and
call to mind the ruined hamlet
that was once
the Home of Kings.

Itu kwan

她总是
知道什么时候
能用浆过的旧单子
给别人的孩子做襁褓

多杜阿的挂彩棕榈树：
她正把
刚洗的新单子
挂起来晒干

随遇而安，讲
你的故事。它们
会让你相信所有的
屋檐都能遮风雨

阿库尔，好姐姐，
谁会愿意在暴风雨天
站在树下面

所以
你
不应该触动
我
去悼挽伟大的祖先
让我缅怀那些倾颓的茅庐
先帝们曾经的家园。

伊图宽

ma
Adze saw o aa
na
Adze asa wo

摩

阿迪仄挚噢啊

呐

阿迪仄挚噢哦

（黄景路　译）

And now the poets speak

Amanda Hammar

We talk across a small table
about the craft hidden within, and the danger
of holding words too close to the heart.

We are from the same place
and not, and anyway somewhere else right now
asking each other, what is the poetry of home,

who the legitimate poets of home.
Is it about *being* there or being *from* there,
having it always speak to you and through you,

or can we write freely
of other things and places, beyond the impossible weight
of our country's soiled history, its fractured urgencies;

can we write unashamedly
of seemingly ordinary things: midsummer's eve,
a son's necessary leaving, the making of a book.

A poet friend says
'it's not where you come from that counts,
but what you do with where you come from'.

现在诗人们说

［津巴布韦］阿曼达·哈玛

我们谈论，围桌而坐
关于诗艺，以及
词一旦趋向本质有多危险。

此刻这些来自同一个地方
或者不是，或者任何其他地方的我们
正询问彼此，何谓诗歌终点

何谓终极的合法诗人。
是否关于*存在*于彼或*存在*源于彼
它总是向你吐诉和借你而说，

或是我们能自由地抒写
其他事情和地点，除了我们急剧分裂
这污秽的国家历史，无法忍受的重任；

我们能否毫无羞耻地
写下看起来平淡无奇的事件：仲夏的前夜，
一个儿子被迫离开，一本书的制作。

一个诗人朋友说
"问题不在于你来自哪里
而在于你从中有何作为。"

Poets from home:
let our words breathe themselves into the world,
let us speak simply from the honest salt of it all.

诗人来自终极；
让我们的词语在世界里呼吸它们自己，
让我们从它所有诚实的盐中简简单单地说。

（张伟栋　译）

This child!

Beaven Tapureta

Was like self-kicking.

Choosing him, poetry

Like an infant

Wrapped in skin-sensitive clothes, crying there

On my doorstep

Dumped by mother Muse

Cry baby.

On my doorstep

I found him suitable for me.

I took him into my African igloo.

An igloo in which I keep the best,

Save the best,

Where I keep the rest

Of myself away from the prowling devils

The place inside the igloo where I provide

Love unlimited

Rapidly he grew up to become me.

Now he fights inside the igloo,

Freedom he desires

To live a life of his own,

Independent of me his father, yet belonging to me!

This child!

Poetry!

这个孩子！

［津巴布韦］比温·塔普莱塔

曾经像自己踢自己。

选择他，诗歌

像个婴儿

裹在让肌肤敏感的襁褓里，在那里哭泣

被缪斯妈妈弃于

我的门外阶前

哭泣的孩子。

我在门外阶前

发现他适合于我。

我将他送入非洲圆顶茅屋。

在这里，我留存最好之物，

积蓄最好之物，

在这里，我留存

远离邪恶徘徊的那一部分自我

我在茅屋中供给

无限之爱

他迅即成长为我。

如今，他在茅屋中斗争，

渴求自由

以获取自己的生活，

独立于我，他的父亲，但属于我！

这个孩子！

诗歌！

（韩博　译）

Showesia – Poema vivo

Tânia Tomé

Queda-se o corpo neste poema
Uma entrega, entrega-se toda
com um desígnio imenso da semente na flor
despindo os versos um a um no centro deste poema

E onde o som nasce, cresce uma palavra devorando lentamente
as metáforas num gesto iniciado de luz e vida
Existe um tortuoso labirinto por entre as sílabas cheio de lustre
por onde brotam os rios e os lábios no mesmo momento de partida

Amá-las bem depressa, bem devagarinho deve ser o caminho
E a pontuação se eleva na subtileza dos versos,
da métrica, da rima, no âmago do silêncio
E há um desejo insano de desfigurar a branca página,
Com cor do olhar que percorre intenso para o outro lado do espelho
onde o mundo acontece sua estrela bailante

E dentro das palavras há melodia,
dependurando-se sobre as arestas do verso
e dançando os murmúrios constantes do voo das aves

E o poema ganha rosto:
uma árvore cheia de cabelos ao vento como teias da aranha,
onde nos pés das raízes habitam os sarcófagos diversos no húmus da loucura

诗秀——生动之诗

[莫桑比克] 塔尼娅·托麦

身体坠入此诗
我全身心投入
急切盼望着在花丛中播种
把诗句一行一行地剥除

歌声诞生之地，孕育着一个词语
舒缓地享用着蕴藏在光与生命中的隐喻
充满光泽的音节躲藏在九曲回肠的迷宫中
从那里流出汩汩河水，正如从唇中说出的话语

爱诗之迫切，但爱的道路漫漫而修远
标点符号跃然在诗句里，韵律中，
游刃在诗的灵魂深处
有一种强烈的愿望，
用穿越镜子的眼神之色涂抹在白纸上
你的舞蹈明星此时被世人瞩目

词语之中蕴藏着旋律
悬挂在诗句之上
犹如鸟儿在空中欢唱

诗歌拂过脸庞：
风中的大树挂满秀发宛如蛛网，
树根下的土壤里静静躺着疯狂者的躯骸

E onde as mãos de asas são janelas,
por onde as pupilas escancaram o mundo entre os dedos

在这里双手和翅膀是窗
从这里双眼透过指缝看到了世界

（鲁扬　译）

ዝምታ ቋንቋ ነው

Alemu Tebeje Ayele

ዝምታ ቋንቋ ነው፤
ቋንቋ ነው ዝምታ፤
ድምጽ ወጥቶ
ድምጽ ጠፍቶ፤
ህሊና ሲያወጋ፤
እንደበት ተኝቶ።

በቃላት ጫጫታ፤
ሆሄያት እሩምታ፤
ላላጣ ጭንቅላት፤
የማድመጥ ችሎታ፤
ለሰከነ አእምሮ፤
ለሚገባው ብልህ፤
ድምጽ አልባ ጨዋታ፤
ዝምታ ቋንቋ ነው፤
ቋንቋ ነው ዝምታ፤
ሹሚያ የሌለበት
አንድ ላንድ ጨዋታ።

沉默是语言

［埃塞俄比亚］阿莱姆·特伯热·艾尔

沉默是语言
语言也是沉默
某种声音说出了
某种声音缺席
只有良心在独白
舌头睡得深沉
词语刺耳的噪音
元音的断奏
因为大脑还清醒
听力也健全
因为智力能捕捉它
沉默很好玩。
沉默是一种语言
而且语言本身也是沉默。
一对一的对话中
没有竞争。

（成婴　译自英语）

لا تهدموا الكوخ

فاطمة ناعوت

أحتاجُ شَبحًا
يرتَّبُ خِزانتي
أثوابُ الراحلين في جهةٍ
و الحِنَّاءُ في جهة.

أحتاجُ شبحًا
ينسِّقُ الكتبَ التي غدرتني:
هذه الكومةُ تستحقُّ القَصاصَ
لأنها نخرتْ طُمأنينتي،
لذلك لن أمانعَ في حشوِ آذانِها بالقشِّ
والبنزين.

الشبحُ سيفهمُ بهجتي
عند حرْقِ الأغلفةِ
ببرودةِ النازيين،
وفردِ الأوراقِ تحت الدجاجِ المقليّ
من أجل إبقاءِ الصحونِ النظيفةِ
نظيفةً
بعد أن لوَّثَها العتّينون بمجازاتِهم الرديئة.

أحتاجُ شبحًا
ينزعُ الأزرارَ من حاسوبي
ويمرِّرُ الفأرةَ فوق الجلدِ المتكسِّر
لتلعقَ البثورَ والغُبارَ
والعلاماتِ التي رسمَها العاشقُ

不要毁坏那座小屋

［埃及］法蒂玛·纳乌特

我需要一个精灵
管理我的衣橱
指甲花放在一边
穿过的衣服在另一边理清。

我需要一个精灵
整理那些背叛我的书籍
这一排需要受罚
因为它扰乱了我的平静，
我也会塞着精灵的耳朵
用杂草和汽油。

这个精灵将懂得我的欢乐
在焚烧那些封面时
像纳粹一样冷酷无情，
在把纸张铺在烤鸡下面时
用以保持盘子的洁净。
洁净
在无能的人用其低级演说诋毁之后。

我需要一个精灵
拆除我键盘上的按键
把鼠标从破碎的表面移走
舔舐粉刺和溃烂的伤口
还有留在恋人

فوق ساقِ الحبيبة.

الأشباحُ فضلاءُ
وصامتون
يصوّبون النارَ على الأقزام
الذين يلطّخون الحوائطَ بدمائِهم
حين ينطحونها بالرأسِ كلَّ سبت
لأنهم بغير ظلّ
ذاك أن الطائرَ الضِّليلَ
لا يحطُّ إلا على رؤوسِ الشعراء.
والأقزامُ
يمتنعون.

الأشباحُ خفيفون
لا يشغلونَ الأمكنةَ
ويقتصدون في الهواءِ وفي الزمن،
علماءُ
يحجبونَ الشمسَ عن قِصارِ القامة
لأن سيقانَهم المُبتَسرةَ
تُفسدُ لوحةَ النور والظِّلال،
وحكماءُ
تنصتوا على الصَّبيّة والفتى
جوارَ الساقية العجوز
ـ لو لم يكن بك عليّ غضبٌ لا أبالي!
فقال: بي !
ونهضَ إلى الكوخِ فبكتْ،
أصغرُهم
صالحَها بوردةٍ
ومسحَ على جديلتِها،

腿上的印迹。

精灵都很忠诚
他们沉默不语
把枪口对准侏儒
因为侏儒血污墙壁
每周六都头撞精灵
但精灵无影无踪。
迷途的鸟儿
只能栖息在诗人的头顶。
侏儒们
避而不见。

精灵们轻如薄纱
不占空间
节约空气和时间,
他们是学者
使侏儒难见阳光
只因他们的小脚
践踏了明暗清晰的画面,
他们是智者
倾听女孩和男孩的对话
位于古老水车旁边
——如果你不为我疯狂,我不在乎!
他说:我已疯狂!
然后他走向小屋　女孩哭泣,
最年幼的精灵
送上玫瑰安慰
抚摸着她的发辫

وكبيرُهم
رفع السَّبابةَ مُنذرًا:
لا تهدموا الكوخَ
به شاعر.

年长精灵
伸出手指警告：
不要毁坏那座小屋
有位诗人住在里面。

（刘炼，刘宝莱　译）

I dance to know who I am

Lebogang Mashile

I.

I dance to know who I am

When I am in motion

I move to find the rhythm

That permeates this commotion

This body is a pen

Its movements are words

Every dance is a tale

I write about this world

It is the physical expression of thoughts

Intertwined with flesh

Where melody and ligaments meet

Infused with breath and sweat

I dance to bring light into darkness

I move to understand what lives beneath the skin

I dance to trace the cord that leads

To who I truly am

II.

My body speaks a wordless language

Its movements are philosophy

There's logic to this living instrument

The dancer sculpting clay that breathes

My body speaks a magic language stripping my soul bare

我舞蹈以认识我是谁

［南非］勒布干·马希尔

I

我舞蹈以认识我是谁
当我在运动中
我移动以找到节奏
它渗透在这骚动中
这身体乃是一支笔
它的运动是词语
每场舞都是传说
我书写这世界
它是思想得到物质的表达
与肉体相交织
那里旋律和韧带相会
充满了呼吸和汗水
我舞蹈以将光带入黑暗
我移动以理解皮肤下的事物
我舞蹈以追踪线索
它将我引向真我

II

我的身体说着一种无言的语言
它的运动是哲学
这活生生的乐器有理可循
舞蹈者雕刻着泥土让它呼吸

我的身体说着一种魔语让我的灵魂赤裸

So that the viewer might be seen
I give every part of myself to strangers
And they find themselves in my dreams

My body speaks a loving language
I travel throughout the world via self-study
My voice is formed by limbs in motion
Wordless expression in a world
Where words are currency

Dance is the intimate exchange of information
With inspiration linking two souls through breath
Is it the part of me you take home with you
The unknown you that has been revealed to yourself
We rely on other bodies to make our bodies whole
The entire complete body is a landscape unknown
Dance can heal a body can make a broken body whole
Dance can never leave a body
It gives body to the soul
I dance with my whole self
I dance to make myself whole
I dance to know myself
Because the self is unknown

The fabric of my flesh is threaded with songs
It is embedded with rhythms as fluid as oceans
And just as long
My hearts percussion flows to my feet
As they play notes on the ground

以便观看者被看见
我将自己的每部分都给予陌生人
而他们发现自己在我的梦里

我的身体说着一种爱的语言
我游遍了世界通过自我钻研
我的声音形成于运动中的肢体
无言的表达在一个
词语才是硬通货的世界中

舞蹈是亲密的沟通消息
伴随着灵感让两颗灵魂由呼吸而相连
你携带回家的部分的我
可否是未知的你已向你自己敞开？
我们依赖于别人的身体以使得我们的身体完整
完全完备的身体是一片未知的风景
舞蹈能医治身体能使破碎的身体完整
舞蹈永远也不能离开身体
它把身体送给灵魂
我与我的整个自己舞蹈
我舞蹈以使得自己完整
我舞蹈以认识自己
因为自我尚是未知

我肉体的丝织品织满了歌
它嵌满了节奏流动如海洋
正如很久以前
我心的跳动流到了我的双脚
正当它们在地上演奏乐符

At once linking past and present
Memory
Magic
Image
Soul and sound
We can read each others bodies
To reveal the fine print of energy
The cord that pulls the power of movement
Throughout our human superstring
Rituals in constant transformation
Create a cultural symphony
Life is moving to the soundtrack of time
Dance is an act of remembering
Humanity is a collective body divine
My dance is my offering

I could use a million words to say
What my body can with one move
My language is physical
Primal
Not primitive
The language I live and love
Is the language I choose
I am a dancer who thinks
A thinker who dances
Movements infused with the ideas in my mind
My body is designed to absorb information
I wouldn't trade my mind for an engineer's mind
My body is a text in constant communication

马上就连通了过去和现在
记忆
魔术
形象
灵魂和声响
我们能够阅读彼此的身体
启开能量精美的印记
牵引运动力的绳子
贯穿于我们人类的超弦
持续变形中的仪式
创造了文化的交响乐
生命正移向时间的音轨
舞蹈是一种回忆的行为
人性是一个集体的身体它神圣
我的舞蹈是我的献祭

身体轻轻的一个移动
说出来要千言万语
我的语言是身体的
原始的
不是初级的
我生活和爱的语言
是我选择的语言
我是一个思想着的舞蹈者
一个舞蹈着的思想者
运动渗透了我心中的观念
身体被设计好了吸收信息
我不会把我心跟一个工程师交换
我的身体是一篇文章在持续沟通

I wouldn't trade my mind for an executive's mind
Even though the lows are low
And the highs are high
Even though after the show
No one sees the loneliness inside

My body speaks a loving language
Channeling words from my pen
Flying high up above
Dance is an intimate exchange
An infinite connection
Dance is an act of love

我不会把我心跟一个执行官交换
即便低者低
高者高
即便在演出之后
没有人看见孤独的里面

我的身体说着一种爱的语言
从我的笔管流出词语
高高地飞起
舞蹈是一个亲密的交换
一个无止境的关联
舞蹈是一个爱的行为

（周伟驰　译）

cricket concerto

Nii Ayikwei Parkes

the ghosts have cast their vote
they must have
the ballot boxes are obese

off the fat of skeletons
the bones of logic have been broken
nine hundred and six

of oseikrom's six hundred
humans have voted
after all who said only men can vote?

the crickets have been crying foul
fowl since night began to fall

the western observers say it's not free and fair
we say our ancestors have spoken
they say we have misused the paper

we say our trees are important
they say we can't count
we point at leaves on the bushes

蛐蛐协奏曲

［加纳］奈伊·阿伊克维·帕克斯

鬼魂们已经投了票
他们一定投了
票箱已拥挤不堪

从肥胖的骨架中
迸出了逻辑的骨头
六百个奥赛克姆①人

投出了九百零六票
毕竟，谁说
只有人才能投票

夜幕降临，蛐蛐们叫嚷着不公
鸡鸭也来凑热闹

西方观察家说：不自由，缺公正
我们说祖宗们也发了话
他们说我们错用了选票

我们说树木很重要
他们说我们不会计数
我们指点乱草片片

---

① 加纳南部地名。译注。

133

they call it a rigged election
we say the gods willed it
whoever wins we will dance

they say we won't hear reason
we ask them what song the crickets sang last night

who said only men can vote?
the ancestors have questions too
but traders on wall street are screaming figures

drowning ancestral cries in waves of inequality
the crickets of oseikrom
played a concerned concerto tonight

the banjo twanged with the weight of debt
the ghosts applauded like puppets

did you hear them?

他们称选举舞弊
我们说神愿如此
不论谁赢，都将跳舞

他们说我们听不进道理
我们问：蛐蛐昨夜唱了什么小曲儿

谁说只有人才能投票
祖宗也有此问
但华尔街的滑头尖声惊叫

想用大嗓门盖住先人的呼号
今夜，奥赛克姆的蛐蛐们
要一起合奏，有所应对

鬼魂鼓掌如木偶
琴弦纠缠了债权

你有没听见？

（姜涛　译）

The Return

Kofi Anyidoho

I:

In my loneliness   I looked upon the Primeval World
And I said to myself: I'll make me a New World
                Filled with Gods and Goddesses

And I dressed the Gods in Glory   the Goddesses in Splendour
Gave them infinite power over all things in Creation:

But the Gods let me down.

They soiled their Glory
With passions unfit for Dogs

II:

And in my Onlyliness   I looked upon the wasted world of Gods
And I said to myself: I'll make me a Newer World
                I'll people it all with HumanBeings

I filled the Earth with Abundance of Life
I kept the Mystery of Eternity
Away from the HumanMind
Lest the fate of the Gods befall the HumanKind.

Exchanging Eternal Peace for Eternal Strife
The fruitfulness of the Earth

归来

[加纳] 科菲·阿尼多赫

I

在我的孤独中　　我回顾远古的世界
我对自己说：　　我将为自己创造一个新世界
　　　　　　　　充满了男神和女神

我把男神装扮得辉煌　　女神装扮得华丽
给予他们超过所有造物的无穷力量：

但众神让我失望。

他们玷污了他们的辉煌
用不适于小人们的热情

II

在我的孤独中　　我回顾神的荒凉的世界
我对自己说：　　我将为自己创造一个更新的世界
　　　　　　　　我将让它住满了人类

我让大地充满丰富的生命
我保守着永生的秘密
远远离开人类
以免让诸神的命运加到人类身上。

用永恒的平静代替永恒的冲突
大地的富足

For the barrenness of Death.

III:
Call back here those Old Drummers

Give them back those broken drums with nasal twangs
Let them put New Rhythms to the Loom
And weave New Tapestries for your Gliding Feet.

The Birth of a New World demands the Graceful Dance of Life.

Now there is still some Laughter in your Souls
Your feet with skill must teach your Hearts
to weave the Graceful Dance of Life.
             the Ancestral Premordial Dance of Birth.

代替死亡的贫瘠

III
把那些年老的鼓手们召回到这里

交还给他们鼻音浓重的破鼓
让他们把新的韵律放进织布机
为你移动的双脚织出新的花毯。

新世界的诞生需要生命优美的舞蹈。

现在仍有一些笑声在你的灵魂中
你熟练的双脚必须教会你的心
排练优美的生命之舞。
　　　　　祖传的原始出生之舞。

（张曙光　译）

139

These hands

Makhosazana Xaba

These hands know putrid pus from oozing wounds.
They know the musty feel of varying forms of faecal formations.

They know the warmth of gushing blood from gaping bodily spaces.
They know of mucus sliding out of orifices.

These hands remember the metallic feel of numerous guns when the telling
click was heard.
They recall the rumbling palm embrace over grenades, ready for the release
of destruction.

These hands will never forget the prickling touch of barbed wire on
border fences.
These hands can still recall the roughness of tree leaves that served as toilet paper
in bushes far away.

These hands have felt pulsating hearts over extended abdomens
They know the depth of vaginas, the opening mouths of wombs,
They know the grasp of minute, minute-old clenched fists.

These hands have squeezed life's juices from painful pounding
breasts.
These hands have made love, producing vibrations from receiving
lovers.

这些手

[南非] 马克霍萨萨纳·萨巴

这些手知晓淤血伤口流出的臭脓。
它们知晓不同排泄物的霉味。

它们知晓大开的躯壳中血流的汩汩的暖意。
它们知晓从洞孔黏液滑出。

这些手牢记报时钟响后手握枪支的金属味。
它们回想起公开毁灭时刻怀揣手榴弹嘀嘀鸣响的掌心。

这些手不会忘记在带刺电网的边境线处锥心的刺痛。
这些手仍记住蹲伏远处灌木丛时树叶当手纸时的粗糙。

这些手已感受被剖腹时跳动的心脏
它们知晓阴道的长度，子宫的开口，
它们知晓分秒紧握拳头。

这些手已从爱人乳房的拍击中挤出生命的汁液。
这些手做过爱，与爱恋的情侣们心有灵犀。

These hands have pressed buttons, knobs and switches.
They have turned screws, and wound clocks, steered wheels and dug holes.
Held instruments, implements and ligaments.
Moulded monuments, created crafts, healed hearts.

These hands now caress the keyboard, fondle pens that massage papers,
Weaning fear, weaving words,
wishing with every fingerprint, that this relationship will last forever.

这些手曾解开纽扣，摁下旋钮和开关。
它们曾拧过螺丝，上过发条钟，开车和挖洞。
修理器械，工具和韧带
浇铸纪念碑，制造游船，治愈心脏。

这些手现在抚摸键盘，抚弄使纸页皱巴的圆珠笔，
给恐惧断奶，编织词语，
用每一个指纹来祝福，这样的关系永不会改变。

（叶美　译）

III   Oppression and Resistance

Words fly like stones, like bullets, like flags in these poems that challenge and observe life on this continent and outside of it. Many of the poets that we would have included now live elsewhere in the world due to the terrible repression they felt in their home countries. Others have left to pursue opportunities awarded by immigration. If the personal is political, the political is often deeply personal. Women wield the pen like swords, carving themselves into the totem of history, and roles are changed and rearranged as the universal genius, restless, hungry and resilient writes itself into the world's memory of humanity, and the world's understanding of what it means to say: I am an African.

III 压迫和反抗

语言如石块、子弹与旗帜跳跃鼓荡在诗歌里，既挑战又注视着这块大陆的里里外外。因为祖国压抑的政治环境，许多我们选录的诗人如今置身海外。更有一些移民海外寻求发展机会。如果个人是政治性的，那政治性就是深刻的个性。女诗人以笔为剑，把自己刻进历史的图腾里；角色变化与变迁，天赋、鼓噪、饥饿与坚韧写进人文的记忆里。全世界都在聆听：我是非洲人。

From the sidelines

Chirikuré Chirikuré

we watched from the sidelines
hundreds of them marching
determination written on their faces
placards screaming their message

we watched from the sidelines
as police approached from the other end
wearing awe striking Israeli riot gear
AK 47 rifles spelling out their purpose

we watched from the sidelines
as placards clashed with guns
determination fizzled into flight
and the police strolled back to base

an abandoned placard fluttered past us
its desperate message still legible:
   "please we beg you
   reduce bread price"

站在边上看

[津巴布韦] 齐里克热·齐里克热

我们站在边上看
他们好几百号人在行进
决定写在他们的脸上
标语尖喊着他们的要求

我们站在边上看
警察从另一边冲来
全副以色列防暴武装，恐怖又醒目
AK47枪拼写出他们的来意

我们站在边上看
标语和枪扭打在一起
决心灰飞烟灭
而警察踱步回到驻地

一张散落的标语飞舞着飘过
绝望的要求依然字迹分明：
　　　"求求你我们求你们了
　　　降一降面包的价格"

（成婴　译）

No serenity here

Keorapetse Kgositsile

An omelette cannot be unscrambled. Not even the one prepared in the crucible of 19th century sordid European design.

When Europe cut up this continent into little pockets of its imperialist want and greed it was not for aesthetic reasons, nor was it in the service of any African interest, intent, or purpose.

When, then, did the brutality of imperialist appetite and aggression evolve into something of such ominous value to us that we torture, mutilate, butcher in ways hideous beyond the imagination, rape women, men, even children and infants for having woken up on what we now claim, with perverse possessiveness and territorial chauvinism, to be our side of the boundary that until only yesterday arrogantly defined where a piece of one European property ended and another began?

In my language there is no word for *citizen*, which is an ingredient of that 19th century omelette. That word came to us as part of the package that contained the bible and the rifle. But moagi[①], resident, is there and it has

---

① seTswana word for resident.

这里不平静

[南非] 凯奥拉佩策·考斯尔

一只煎蛋无法被还原。更不必说一只在19世纪肮脏的欧式坩埚里做出来的煎蛋。

当欧洲将这片大陆分割到它帝国主义贪婪的小口袋里，它不是出于美学的理由，也不曾服务于非洲人的利益、意图和目的。

那么，是什么时候，帝国主义贪欲和侵略的残忍，演变成我们这样一种险恶的价值观呢？即，我们以超出想象的种种可怖的方式，折磨、破坏、屠杀，强奸妇女、男人、甚至儿童和婴儿，因为我们在这个我们现在宣布为我们的边界上甫一觉醒就染上了蛮横无理的占有欲和地区沙文主义，而这个边界直到昨天还被傲慢地划分着，分成一块又一块欧洲的私产。

在我的语言里，没有词对应于"公民"，它是那个19世纪煎蛋的原料之一。这个词是作为那装有圣经和来福枪的包裹的一部分降临于我们的。而莫阿吉①，居民，它在那里，无关于你在你当下生活着的

---

① 梭托语，意为"居民"。原注。

nothing to do with any border or boundary you may or
may not have crossed before waking up on the piece of
earth where you currently live.

Poem, I know you are reluctant to sing
when there is no joy in your heart
but I have wondered all these years
why you did not or could not give
answer when Langston Hughes who
wondered as he wandered asked
what happens to a dream deferred

I wonder now
why we are some
where we did not aim
to be. Like my sister
who could report from any
where people live
I fear the end of peace
and I wonder if
that is perhaps why
our memories of struggle
refuse to be erased
our memories of struggle
refuse to die

we are not strangers

这片土地上醒来之前也许穿过或不曾穿过的任何国境或分界线。

诗呵，我知道你不愿歌唱
当你心中没有欢乐
但这么多年来我总想知道
为何你没有或无法回答
当兰斯顿·休斯①疑惑
和徘徊着，问
是什么让一个梦想延搁？

现在我疑惑
为何我们身处
我们并未追求的地方
像我的姐妹
她能从人们生活的
任何地方发回报道
我忧心于和平的结束
疑心这或许就是
为什么
我们抗争的记忆
拒绝被抹除
我们抗争的记忆
拒绝死亡

对于和平的结束

---

① 兰斯顿·休斯（1902—1967），美国黑人诗人，此节最后一句出自他的诗《迟到的梦》（A Dream Deferred）。译注。

to the end of peace
we have known women widowed
without any corpses of husbands
because the road to the mines
like the road to any war
is long and littered with casualties
even those who still walk and talk

when Nathalie, whose young eyes know things, says
there is nothing left after wars, only other wars
wake up whether you are witness or executioner
the victim, whose humanity you can never erase,
knows with clarity more solid than granite
that no matter which side you are on
any day or night an injury to one
remains an injury to all

somewhere on this continent
the voice of the ancients warns
that those who shit on the road
will meet flies on their way back
so perhaps you should shudder under the weight
of nightmares when you consider what
thoughts might enter the hearts of our neighbours
what frightened or frightening memories might jump up
when they hear a South African accent

even the sun, embarrassed, withdraws her warmth
from this atrocious defiance and unbridled denial

我们并不陌生
我们知道那些成为寡妇的女人
连丈夫的尸体都得不到
因为通向矿井的路
就像通向任何战争的路
漫长而事故丛生
而他们仍然走着聊着

当娜塔莉（她有一双年轻却懂事的眼睛）说，
战争不会留下任何东西，除了更多的战争
无论你是见证人还是刽子手，醒来吧
受害者的人性你无法抹杀
他们比花岗岩还坚实地懂得
无论你处于哪一方
任何时间，对一个人的伤害
也会留给所有人

在这片大陆的某处
有一句古老的警告
谁在路上拉屎
谁就会在回来时遇上苍蝇
因此当你想到我们邻居心中可能的念头
你或许会被压在沉重的梦魇之下发抖
当他们听到一个南非人的口音
又会跳出多么可怕的或受惊的记忆

这种理应约束我们的联系
对它恶毒的藐视和不受控制的否认

of the ties that should bind us here and always
and the night will not own any of this stench
of betrayal which has desecrated our national anthem
so do not tell me of NEPAD or AU
do not tell me of SADC
and please do not try to say shit about
ubuntu[①] or any other such neurosis of history

again I say, while I still have voice,
remember, always
remember that you are what you do,
past any saying of it

our memories of struggle
refuse to be erased
our memories of struggle
refuse to die

my mothers, fathers of my father and me
how shall I sing to celebrate life
when every space in my heart is surrounded by corpses?

---

① Zulu word describing the African metaphor: a person is a person is a
person because of other people.

甚至连太阳也窘迫地撤回她的光芒
而夜也会无法容忍这亵渎了
我们国歌的背叛的恶臭
所以不要对我说NEPAD^①或AU^②
不要对我说SADC^③
也请不要讲什么乌班图^④或
任何其他这类历史神经症的狗屎

我再次说，当我还能发出声音，
记住，始终记住
你做了什么，你就是什么，
这胜过任何格言

我们抗争的记忆
拒绝被抹除
我们抗争的记忆
拒绝死亡

我的母亲，祖父和我
当我心中每一处都被尸体包围
我如何才能吟咏和赞颂生命？

---

① 非洲发展新型伙伴关系（New Partnership for Africa's Development）计划的英文缩写。译注。
② 非洲联盟（African Union）的英文缩写。译注。
③ 南部非洲发展共同体（Southern African Development Community）的英文缩写。译注。
④ 原文为祖鲁语，意指人与人之间的社会联结，在非洲人的世界观里，这被视为个体存在的基础。作者在这里抨击的是这个词被滥用以服务于种种私利的状况。原注。

whose thousand thundering voices shall I borrow to shout

once more: *Daar is kak in die land!* [1]

---

[1] Afrikaans phrase that means that there is shit in the country.

我该借用谁的雷鸣般响亮的嗓音
再次喊出：*这个国家里那些狗屎！* [①]

[①] 原文为南非荷兰语，根据作者解释，他以这句街头土语，想表达出对当今南非政治体制和社会结构中所存在的腐败堕落状况的强烈忧愤之情。原注。

Friends, Citizens, Captives

Obododimma Oha

I

"To keep Nigeria one is a task that must be done"
-- Nigeria's civil war slogan

Jack of the Union britished
Captives of the Niger, ancient peoples proud
To be different but free

The citizen the captive now
The captive the Nigerian forever
Living together against their will
Perishing together against their will

Jack was the union, tin-faced
To keep Nigeria one without knowing why
The boiling hotpots of Jos tell angrily
A middle belt not tight, never will

朋友、公民、囚徒

[尼日利亚]奥波多迪玛·奥哈

I

"维护尼日利亚统一是一项必须完成的任务"
——尼日利亚内战宣言①

大不列颠的杰克同化
尼日尔②俘虏，这古老种族曾自豪于
不同而又自由。

现在公民意味着俘虏
俘虏永远是尼日利亚人
违心地一起生活
违心地一起毁灭

杰克曾是联邦，长着罐头脸
维持尼日利亚统一但不知道为什么
乱成沸粥般的乔斯③愤怒地诉说
中部统一不了，将永不统一

---

① 从1967年到1970年，尼日利亚爆发了一场空前惨烈的战争——尼日利亚内战，这场战争造成了200万—300万人的死亡和空前的饥馑，产生了深远的国际影响，留下了许多至今尚未消除的后遗症。译注。
② 这里的尼日尔，并非与尼日利亚毗邻的尼日尔国家，而指尼日利亚成为现代国家之前在此居住的土著种族。尼日利亚，即为尼日尔河流经的土地。译注。
③ 乔斯（Jos），尼日利亚中部城市，是高原州首府，也是该州最大的城市，那里南北方民族、穆斯林和基督徒交错杂居。新世纪以来，尼日利亚中部地区暴力冲突不断。译注。

Jack wins away
When he loses at home

II

Jos of the just
Always cold, too cold
So bloodshed makes her hot

Can't read the expressions
On the brows of the tired hills
For the fog weighs heavily
On the harms of the harmattan

A citizen wakes
In the captivity of his own stories
A neighbour's presence that sours
In mutual hate & easy death

Jos, just the climax
Takes us to the beginning

杰克赢了。
而他在国内遭到了失败^①

II

公正的乔斯
一贯冷，太冷^②
流血令她发热

不要去解读山脊倦怠
的表情
浓雾笼罩
在热风^③的废墟上。

在自我虚构的捆缚中
公民醒来
邻里关系变得尖锐
在相互仇恨与轻生中

乔斯，正是这沸点
带我们返回到起点

---

① 所谓国内失败，指英国联邦内北爱尔兰的六个郡要求独立引发
的争端至今都没解决。译注。
② 据作者解说，"harm of harmattan" 隐喻"乔斯这个城市的暴力
与大屠杀"。在harmattan季节期间，尼日利亚极度寒冷，从效果上
来看，气候寒冷造成的损害，与暴力对人类财产与生命造成的实际
损害有类似性。译注。
③ harmattan，（自撒哈拉沙漠吹向非洲西北海岸）干燥含尘之热
风。这里指乔斯这个城市的大屠杀。译注。

When Jack britished someone's right
Not to nation with the other.

当杰克强化某人的权力

不是与他人一起组建国家。

（余旸　译）

Death in the Dawn

Wole Soyinka

Traveller, you must set out
At dawn. And wipe your feet upon
The dog-nose wetness of earth.

Let sunrise quench your lamps, and watch
Faint brush pricklings in the sky light
Cottoned feet to break the early earthworm
On the hoe. Now shadows stretch with sap
Not twighlight's death and sad prostration

This soft kindling, soft receding breeds
Racing joys and apprehensions for
A naked day, burdened hulks retract,
Stoop to the mist in faceless throng
To wake the silent markets – swift, mute
Processions on grey byways...

On this
Counterpane, it was —
Sudden winter at the death
Of dawn's lone trumpeter, cascades
Of white feather-flakes, but it proved
A futile rite. Propition sped
Grimly on, before.
The right foot for joy, the left, dread

黎明中的死亡

[尼日利亚] 沃莱·索因卡

旅人，你必须在黎明
出发。用大地的狗鼻湿
擦擦你的脚。

让日出熄了你的灯，看看
天光中微弱的笔触
它的脚友好地唤醒了锄端的
蚯蚓。现在影子展开的是活力
不是曙光的消逝和神伤疲惫

这轻轻的点火，谦和的生育
喜和忧角着力，要迎来
一个坦荡的白天，沉重的弃船后拉，
坠入薄雾，坠入无名的人群
唤醒沉默的集市——无名小道上
那匆忙无声的行列……

在这
床单上，原来是——
冬天在黎明的孤独号手死亡时
突然降临，白色片羽
漂如飞瀑，但证明
都是无意义的仪式。之前，
祭物只顾加速前进。
右脚追逐快乐，左脚迎向恐惧

And the mother prayed, Child
May you never walk
When the road waits, famished.

Traveller you must set forth
At dawn.
I promise marvels of the holy hour
Presages as the white cock's flapped
Perverse impalement – as who would dare
The wrathful wings of man's Progression…

But such another Wraith! Brother,
Silenced in the startled hug of
Your invention — is this mocked grimace
This closed contortion – I?

母亲祈祷着，而孩子
你能否永不迈步
当道路等着你，如饥似渴。

旅人你必须在黎明
出发。
我保证神圣时刻的奇迹
会兆示为白公鸡被突然围住时
着急忙慌的样子——谁又敢挑战
人类前进那愤怒的翅膀。

但兄弟，那会是另一种显灵！
被你的虚构悍然抱住时
仍默不作声——这嘲弄的鬼脸，
紧紧的扭曲——是我吗？

（席亚兵　译）

Slaughterhouse of Sanity

Stanley Onjezani Kenani

*For Jack Mapanje, upon seeing for the first time the
Mikuyu Detention Centre where the poet was jailed
for three years without trial*

sanity after sanity
brutally butchered by the mighty
the poet's lines made to bleed
   in this slaughterhouse

stanza upon stanza shackled
shell-shocked to the verge of
   insanity
ball-point pens ruthlessly gagged
   in this slaughterhouse

hope hanged on a rope
spirit stretched to snapping point
the poem stood its ground
   in this slaughterhouse

理智的屠宰场

[马拉维] 斯坦利·昂热扎尼·克那尼

给杰克·玛潘哲，第一次与诗人相遇是在他未
经审判，但已监禁三年的迈库钰拘留中心。

理智之后的理智
被强大的力量残酷屠杀
诗人的诗句导致流血
　　在这个屠宰场

节节诗行被束缚
被轰炸至疯狂的
边缘
圆珠笔被无情地塞住
　　在这个屠宰场

仅存的一线希望，渺茫
精神被挖掘至崩溃的临界点
诗歌站立它自己的地面
　　在这个屠宰场

（张伟栋　译）

显像 3　胡项城

（Appearance III　Hu Xiangcheng）

እንባ-አልባ እንባ

Alemu Tebeje Ayele

በእንባ ሙላት
እንባው ደርቆ፤
በአንባ ቅርበት
እንባው 'ርቆ፤
ቢስተዋልም ጥርሱ ስቆ፤
ሰው ያለቅሳል
ሰው እያሉ ተደብቆ፤
በእንባ-አልባ እንባ ተንሰቅስቆ።

ብቸኝነት ከብቻኘነት
መዳረሻ ካደረሰው፤
መች ነው በንባው?!
በኡኡታው?!
ልቦና እርሙን የሚያወጣው!
ታጥቦን እንጂ በእንባ-አልባ እንባ፤
አልቅሶ እንጂ በፈገግታው፤
በሰው መሃል ሰው ሳየው።

无泪之泪

[埃塞俄比亚] 阿莱姆·特伯热·艾尔

泪水泛滥
眼泪干涸
眼泪这么近
眼泪又如此远。
人笑的时候在哭
偷偷躲起来
呜咽着无泪之泪。
如果寂寞让他
达到孤独的极点
一个男人什么时候为他的悲哀找到终结
  流泪哭号
洗面的却是无泪之泪
  含笑哭泣着
混在人群中，都看到他没哭？

（成婴　译自英语）

Who will wash my feet?

Makhosazana Xaba

Who will wash my feet?
My tears dried before 1990.
My thirst is unknown.
My hunger is not for food.
My wounds are inside.
My womb weeps silences.
My nipples watch the soil
to safeguard those
who travelled through me.
My memories run in my veins.
My cracked and dry feet
have never touched a shoe
or the floor of any office.
But I also like the idea
 of someone washing my feet.

谁会给我洗脚？

［南非］马克霍萨萨纳·萨巴

谁会给我洗脚？
我的眼泪在1990年前干涸。
我的口渴无人知。
我的饥饿不是因为食物。
我的伤口全长在内心。
我的子宫静默地哭泣。
我的乳头凝视土壤
以保护那些
旅行此地的人们。
我的记忆在静脉里奔淌。
我噼啪干裂的双脚
从未穿上鞋
或踏入任何办公室的地板。
但是我仍乐意
有人给我洗脚。

（叶美　译）

Anguish longer than sorrow

Keorapetse Kgositsile

If destroying all the maps known
would erase all the boundaries
from the face of this earth
I would say let us
make a bonfire
to reclaim and sing
the human person

Refugee is an ominous load
even for a child to carry
for some children
words like *home*
could not carry any possible meaning
but
displaced
border
refugee
must carry dimensions of brutality and terror
past the most hideous nightmare
anyone could experience or imagine

Empty their young eyes
deprived of a vision of any future
they should have been entitled to
since they did not choose to be born

痛苦比悲伤更长久

[南非] 凯奥拉佩策·考斯尔

假使销毁所有已知的地图
可以从这个地球表面
抹除所有边界
我要说让我们
燃起篝火
复归且歌唱
有人性的人

*难民*是一种不祥的重负
即便是一个孩子来承担
对于一些孩子
家这样的词
已无法承载任何可能的意义
然而
流离
边境
难民
必然带有残酷和恐怖的一面
超过任何人可能经历或想象的
最令人惊骇的梦魇

他们稚嫩的两眼空空
被剥夺了他们本应拥有的
任何未来的想象
因为他们并未选择落生于

where and when they were
Empty their young bellies
extended and rounded by malnutrition
and growling like the well-fed dogs of some
with pretensions to concerns about human rights
violations

Can you see them now
stumble from nowhere
to no
where
between
nothing
and
nothing

Consider
the premature daily death of their young dreams
what staggering memories frighten and abort
the hope that should have been
an indelible inscription in their young eyes

Perhaps
I should just borrow
the rememberer's voice again
while I can and say:
to have a home is not a favour

他们所在的何时何地
他们幼小的肚腹空空
被营养不良拉扯和包围
低吼着像某些
自命关心人权的人
喂得饱饱的狗

现在你能看见他们吗
蹒跚着，从无地
到无
地
在
虚无
与虚无
之间

想想
他们年少的梦想日常的夭折
多么骇人的记忆惊吓并流产了希望
那本应是他们年少的眼中
不可消除的印迹啊

也许
我正应再次借用
那铭记者的声音
当我能够并说出：
拥有一个家不是一种恩惠

（冷霜　译）

The wall's lament

Shabbir Banoobhai

I have no strength
besides the strength you give me.

I have no hope
besides the hope you place in me.

I have no will
besides the will with which you build me.

I have no courage to match your fear
now cemented in the concrete within me.

When you are blind I become blind.
When you allow light into your heart

a gate I had almost forgotten existed
opens, deep in a recess in my spine.

So really, I have no sight at all
yet I see what you see in me.

I have no dream, not even
if there is barrenness around me

to find out if there are orchards

墙之哀歌

［南非］沙比尔·巴努海

除去你所赐予
我再无力量。

除去你所置予
我再无希望。

除去你所塑予
我再无意志。

我没有勇气与你此刻
砌筑于我体内的恐惧较量。

当你盲时我亦盲。
当你允许光线射入内心

一道我几乎忘记其存在的门
洞开，在我脊柱凹陷的深处。

所以，我其实并无所见
我之所见仅为你于我之所见。

我并无梦想，即便
贫瘠环绕于我

我也不去寻找

growing on the other side.

I cannot live unless you live within me.
I cannot die even if you dismantle me

unless something in you
that created me, dies with me.

But it is easier for you
to recreate me in other forms

call me by gentler names
that conceal the harm they perpetrate

than to allow me to vanish without a trace
so fearful are you of losing an essence

you believe only survives
within you because of me.

I have no strength
besides the strength you give me.

I have no hope
besides the hope you place in me.

I have no will
besides the will with which you build me.

别处是否另有果园。

若你不能与共我便无以生存。
若你不能与共我便无以死亡

除非你摧毁我之时
亦创造我。

但于你而言
以别样形式重造我

为隐藏恶行之害
而用文雅之名称谓我

远比让我消失得了无痕迹更易
你为失去本质而如此恐惧

你相信你之存续
因我而存续。

除去你所赐予
我再无力量。

除去你所置予
我再无希望。

除去你所塑予
我再无意志。

I have no courage to match your fear
now cemented in the concrete within me.

Attempting to separate
your hopes from your fears

you inevitably convert
your hopes to your fears.

Trying to be free
through separation

you lose your freedom
through isolation;

for the beauty of a cloud
does not lie in the cloud

it lies in drought;
the beauty of the day

does not lie in the light
it lies in the darkness of night;

the beauty of infinity
lies in rootedness.

Can you not see the futility
of striving for perfection

我没有勇气与你此刻
砌筑于我体内的恐惧较量。

你试图将希望
剥离于恐惧

却必然将希望
转化为恐惧。

你试图借隔离
换取自由

却因孤绝
失去自由；

因为云之美
不在于云

而在于干旱；
日之美

不在于光线
而在于夜之黑暗；

无限之美
在于根深蒂固。

难道你看不见
于不完美之不完美理解

with a flawed understanding
of imperfection?

Can you not hear the disquiet
in the very silence you are creating?

I have no strength
besides the strength you give me.

I have no hope
besides the hope you place in me.

I have no will
besides the will with which you build me.

I have no courage to match your fear
now cemented in the concrete within me.

Some gifts have no meaning
when we possess them entirely;

and some ailments are themselves
the only cure for the illness they constitute.

So unless blindness itself becomes the cure
for a flawed sight, you will rebuild me

in your heart, even when you reduce me

于努力渴求完美
之无益?

难道你听不见
你于静寂创造之嘈杂?

除去你所赐予
我再无力量。

除去你所置予
我再无希望。

除去你所塑予
我再无意志。

我没有勇气与你此刻
砌筑于我体内的恐惧较量。

当我们拥有某些天赋
它们却全然无用;

某些微恙成其自身
唯一的疗法同于病灶。

除非盲目自身
成为盲目的疗法

即便你将我贬作碎瓦

to rubble on the ground.

And if you cannot form me
in the full light of your nightmares

you will form me in the half light
of your hidden fears;

see in the half light of your waking
a bridge fall, in its place a wall;

see in the half light of your sleeping
a mist-like veil enveloping the sun;

see in the half light of your dreaming
the moon reddening, the sky blackening.

O when will you learn
what lies within you lies within me?

O how will you see
what lives beyond me lives beyond you?

I have no strength
besides the strength you give me.

I have no hope
besides the hope you place in me.

你仍于内心将我重塑。

若你未能借梦魇的
充足光线为我赋形

亦会借私藏的恐惧
那半明之光为我赋形。

在你醒来的半明之光中
目睹桥梁轰塌，高墙矗起；

在你睡下的半明之光中
目睹迷雾般的幔帐遮掩太阳；

在你梦见的半明之光中
目睹月亮变红，天空蒙黑。

哦，何时你会明白
何事尽在你我？

哦，怎样你会看见
何事高于你我？

除去你所赐予
我再无力量。

除去你所置予
我再无希望。

I have no will
besides the will with which you build me.

I have no courage to match your fear
now cemented in the concrete within me.

除去你所塑予
我再无意志。

我没有勇气与你此刻
砌筑于我体内的恐惧较量。

（韩博　译）

How ill a poem

Obododimma Oha

How ill could a poem get
When it walks into the rhetoric of the Government House;
A fever of words saying one thing & meaning another
A headache of weary metaphors
A running tummy of badly cooked hyperboles
Some rashes of collocations
And an overtax of syntax.

一首诗能病成啥样？

［尼日利亚］奥波多迪玛·奥哈

一首诗能病成啥样？
当它陷入官样的花言巧语
它发烧，言不由衷
头疼，隐喻苍白
胡乱的夸饰让它拉稀
不当的搭配生疹子
还有那使它虚脱的句法。

（余旸　译）

Wounded dreams

Keorapetse Kgositsile

Amongst the silences of restless nights
My voice wants to break through the shell of words
to name and sing the evidence
of our resolve and will to live
past the glib claims of noble intentions

If you have never walked through
the restless shadows of wounded dreams
beware; the young ones of tomorrow
might curse you by not wanting to remember
anything about your ways because everything
about you leaves a bitter taste in the mouth

Amongst the silences of these restless nights
our dreams refuse the perfumed bandages
that try to hide the depth of their wounds
Our voice yearns for the precision to name
what we are most responsive to
the way our lady of the mutton vindaloo
of my demand said: *Listen here,*
Shorty, this is hell's kitchen
you'll walk out of here tall you hear

Though the present remains
a dangerous place to live

受伤的梦

[南非] 凯奥拉佩策·考斯尔

在不眠之夜的寂静中
我的声音想穿透词语的壳
去命名和歌唱我们
生活的决心和意志的证据
超过高贵意图的肤浅要求

假如你未曾走出
受伤的梦那不眠的阴影
当心；明天的年青人
也许会诅咒你而不愿记住
与你有关的任何事物
因为它们每一样都在嘴里留下苦味

在这些不眠之夜的寂静中
我们的梦拒绝熏香的绷带
遮掩它们伤口的深度
我们的声音渴望精确地命名
我们最热忱的事物
我要香辣羊时
我们的女士说：*听着*
小矮个，这儿是地狱的厨房
你会离开这儿的

尽管此刻留下的是
一个危险的生存空间

cynicism would be a reckless luxury
toxic lies piled high and deodorized
to sound like the most clear signage
showing us the way forward from here

Not that I am dotard enough
to think it could ever be easy
or without pain to do anything
of value. But when I am surrounded
by the din of publicly proclaimed multiple promises
I wonder if we can say with determined resolve
like Fidel: *Never again will pain return*
to the hearts of mothers nor shame to
the souls of all honest South Africans

Though the present is
a dangerous place to live
possibility remains what moves us
we are all involved
indifference would simply be
evidence of the will to die
or trying to straddle some fence
that no one has ever seen

together we can and must
rehabilitate our wounded dreams
to reclaim and nourish the song

冷嘲热讽仍属鲁莽而奢侈
有毒的谎言堆积成山还被除味
听上去像是最明白的标志
指示我们向前的路

不是我昏聩已极
以为那会多么容易
或能毫不吃力地做任何
有价值的事，而是当我被包围在
公开宣布的多项承诺的喧嚣之中
我不知道我们是否能像菲德尔①那样
斩钉截铁地说：*母亲们的心*
将不再受苦，所有诚实的
南非人的灵魂也不再蒙羞

尽管此刻是
一个危险的生存空间
可能性却保留了那感动我们的事物
我们都参与其中
冷漠将只是
死亡意志的征兆
或不承担责任的企图
没有人能够做到

我们能够而且必须共同
恢复我们受伤的梦
开垦和灌溉我们生气勃勃的

———————————

① 指古巴前领导人菲德尔·卡斯特罗，作者将其原话中的"古巴人"替换为"南非人"。译注。

of the quality of our vibrant being
as evidence of how it is to be alive
past any need for even a single lie

Out of the silences
of these restless nights
my voice wants to break
through the shell of words
and fly to the rooftops
to shout: when we have walked through
the restless shadows of wounded dreams
and come back from tomorrow together
we shall know each other
by the root and texture of our appetite

存在品质之歌
以证明它将怎样充满活力
不需要哪怕一句谎言

在这些不眠之夜的
寂静之上
我的声音想穿透
词语的壳
飞向屋顶
呼喊：当我们走出
受伤的梦不眠的阴影
一起从明天返回
我们将认识彼此
透过我们愿望的表皮和根

（冷霜　译）

The fighter

Hama Tuma

The fire dies down, darkness grows
The butterfly moves away
        to search for death elsewhere.
He hugs his rifle, and broods
        faces of the dead parade before his eyes.
Moist eyes do not hamper memory's vision
As the heart recalls songs of the past
        and the mind conjures images of bright
sunny days.
The rifle kills,
        the rifle saves
He tugs at his inconsistency
        and settles on his "no choice" reasoning.
A hyena howls in the distance
        signalling in the dark a change of mood
He hugs tight the gun
and listens to the fire in his heart
And sees a bright dawn breaking
        moving men and birds to gaiety
To a song of joy
        whose words he knew not yet
But felt himself being stirred.
In the distance, echoes of rifle fire
The present intrudes with death on a platter
He moves with his gun into the night.

战士

[埃塞俄比亚] 哈玛·图玛

火燃尽了，黑暗生长着
蝴蝶飞走
　　　　去探究别处的死亡。
他抱着来复枪，沉思着
　　　　眼前经过的死者的脸。
潮湿的双眼阻止不了记忆的幻象
当内心回想起过去的歌曲
　　　　头脑中浮现出晴朗白昼的
明亮画面。
来复枪屠杀，
　　　　来复枪保命
他拖着他的矛盾
　　　　确定他"没有选择"的理由。
一只鬣狗在远处嚎叫
　　　　于黑暗中传递着情绪的变化
他抱紧那支枪
听着他内心的火焰
看着明亮的黎明出现
　　　　把人和鸟带进欢乐
带进一首喜悦的歌中
　　　　他还不知道它的词句
但感到自己正在被打动。
远处，来复枪回响着
"现在"轻易地伴着死亡侵入
他带枪走入夜里。

（张曙光　译）

201

العفريت

فاطمة ناعوت

غرسَ الشوكةَ في خِصرِها
فتحوّلتُ إلى هيأةِ الجواري:
تجلبُ الماءَ من البئرْ،
وتعدُّ قهوةَ الصُبحِ
ثم تسوّكُ أسنانَه من بقايا الفطورِ،
والنساءْ.

تِكْ تِكْ،
يصفّقُ،
فتنبسطُ له أرضًا
تُنبِتُ القمحَ والشعيرَ والنارنجْ.

تِكْ تِكْ

فتنتفضُ، كصليبٍ مُشرع وسطَ الحقلْ،
خيالَ مآتة
تُفزّعُ الطيرَ وتهشُّ الألسنتيّنَ واللصوصْ،
ثم تُنقّي ماءَ البِركةِ من الدَنَس
كي تغسلَ أصابَعها المبتورةِ بسيفِ الخوارجْ
وتُشهرَ قميصَه فوق صدرِها
ليجفَّ من الدمْ.

تِكْ
فتغدو ناعورةً
تروي أرضَه
وترسمُ فوق صفحةِ القنايةِ

202

恶魔

［埃及］法蒂玛·纳乌特

他在她周围种下荆棘
使她变成奴婢：
她从井里提取清水，
准备早上咖啡
然后清除他残留在牙齿上的早餐碎屑，
还照顾女人。

拍手 拍手
他拍动双手，
她变成一块土地
为他提供小麦，大麦和柑橘。

拍手　拍手
她变成田野里的十字架，
一个稻草人
恐吓飞鸟，乐坏语言学家和盗贼，
她从池塘里取出清水
清洗她被盗匪砍伤的手指
然后把他的衬衫罩在自己的胸前
让血迹晾干。

拍手
她变成水车
灌溉他的土地
在溪流上

دوائرَ وظلالاً
لزومَ اكتمالِ اللوحةِ.

عند الظهرْ
يصفّقُ من جديد
فتنقلبُ أبا قردان
يلقطُ الدودَ من التربة
ويُنقّي خطوطَ القطنِ من اللُّطعِ،
ثُم سمكةً
تجمعُ الطميَ في بطنِها
لتفرغَهُ في حوضٍ الوردِ الشماليّ.

تِكْ تِكْ تِكْ تِكْ تِكْ
فتحولّتْ على إثرِها مُهْرةً
امتطاها
ليتفقّدَ بساتينَه الواسعة
وفي يمينِه سوطُ نيتشه:
شيخ البلد.

الفلاحُ الأشهبُ
تعلّمَ حكمةَ القرويين وطقوسَهم،
روّضَ المرأةَ بقانون العِفريتِ،
ثم اضطجعَ على حافةِ الترعةِ في استراحةِ القيلولة
حدّقَ في عينيها برهةً
فاستوتْ له صبيةً
ضاجعَها
واستولدها طفلةً شهباءَ،
قتلَها.

204

画出
明暗轻快的图画。

中午时分
他再次拍手
她变为一只朱鹭
叼出地里的虫子
啄出棉线中的虫卵，
她又变成鱼
吞噬泥沙
在北方的玫瑰园里将她的胃洗净。

拍手　拍手　拍手　拍手
她变成一匹小骒马
他骑上去
巡视他那巨大的庄园
右手握着尼采的皮鞭：
庄园的主人。

这位老农民
知晓村民的智慧和传统，
依照魔鬼的法则对那女人进行了训练，
然后在水沟边打了一个盹
睁眼看着她的眼睛
她为他变成了一位少女
二人同衾共枕
她生下一个粉红色的女婴，
他杀了她。

جميلةً كانت
ولذا
شخبطَ على وجهها في التصاويرْ
بطبشورٍ أسودَ
إذ ملاحتُها
تكشفُ قبحَ الرفاقْ.

قبل الغروبِ
جفَّ حلقُه
فتكوّرتْ له عِلكةً
لاكَها
ثم
بصقَها،
فتمطّتْ على الرملِ
وتحوّرتْ حواءَ،
ولما اكتملتْ أنوثتُها
نامتْ على رجاءِ القيامةِ.

عند المغرب
انتزع الشوكةَ من لحمِها
فتبخرّتْ.

她长得漂亮
因此
他毁了她的肖像
用的是黑色粉笔
因为她的美丽
使他的同伴显得丑陋。

日落前
他喉咙发干
她为他变成一块口香糖
他咀嚼着
然后
吐出来，
口香糖在沙粒中展开
变成了夏娃，
当她具备了女性的一切
便仅安于转世复活的愿望。

日落时分
他移开荆棘
而她已经蒸发。

（刘炼，刘宝莱　译）

Womanchild

Lebogang Mashile

At 11, she stood on the precipice
With dolls floating between her ears
And new worlds expanding below her waist
Without wings, her body was a prison

At 13, the ocean fell
A bottomless tide ferried her to Daddy's lap
Which no longer had room for a woman
And men whose stares grab
When no one is looking
Below water, her body was a volcano

At 15, she stood unarmed before infantries
Who deemed her terrain to be clean
A predator's wet dream
Without weapons, her body was an invitation

At 17, she was sold to the highest bidder
Her ringed finger a prize
For a husband three times her size
Without warning, her body was a trophy

女人孩

[南非]勒布干·马希尔

十一岁，她站在悬崖上
玩偶娃娃悬荡在两耳之间
新的世界伸展在腰部以下
没有翅膀，她的身体是一座牢房

十三岁，海洋坠落
一场无底潮把她运送给爹地的大腿
那里却没有女人的空间
运送给目光攫人的男人们
即使没有人在看
在水下，她的身体是一座火山

十五岁，她赤手站在步兵的面前
他们视她为要清洗的领地
一个捕食者潮湿的梦
没有武器，她的身体是一个邀请

十七岁，她被卖给最高投标者
对一个体积三倍于她的丈夫
她镶了环的手指是一个奖赏
没有警告，她的身体是一个战利品

（周伟驰 译）

Going down there

Phillippa Yaa de Villiers

This is a letter scratched out by candlelight:
I leave it for all those who are also
confined, painfully pressed, split open.
Those who hold themselves tightly in their hands
so that they will not spill over
and drain away.
Fear eats hope like the night eats the day
leaving only crumbs of stars. Too far away
to be of any help.

I was raped at six, 11, at 13, at 17 and 19
I didn't know I was violated because
where I came from
love was forced and
sometimes hurt.

The frail meat of humankind
can't withstand extremes. We construct ourselves
around ourselves, making of our lives
a shelter.
When you build a house,
you place the window carefully;
when you grow out of a wound,
you see life through
a survivor's eyes.

下到那儿去

［南非］菲丽帕·维利叶斯

这是用烛光拼写出的一封信：
我把它留给所有那些
也被限制、被分裂、痛苦地受到压迫的人。
那些紧紧地用双手抱着自己
免得被掏空
被榨干的人。
恐怖吞噬着希望像夜晚吞噬着白昼
只剩下星星的碎片。太远了
帮不上任何的忙。

我在6岁、11岁、13岁、17岁和19岁时被强奸
我并不知道我是受到了侵犯因为
在我们那儿
爱是被强迫的并且
有时是伤害。

人类脆弱的肉
不能承受极端。我们环绕着自己
把自己构造，把我们的生命
造成一座庇护所。
当你建造房屋，
你会细心地安好窗户；
当你从伤口中成长，
你会用一个幸存者的眼睛
来看生活。

Rapes were my bread: I eat   I understand.
Then later;   I understand,   I eat.
The marks on my house/body/shell are
the keloid memories of
African warriors: scars
deliberately inflicted, a sign of identity.
I read them like Braille.

When they found me I was filthy,
wild and mute. They asked me: what
happened? Compassion unlocked
the cage of memory, and words fell out of me
like the crumbs in Gretel's dark forest,
pebbles of hope,
words
became light
showing me
how to get home.

I am healed now.
But I no longer
look the same.

强奸是我的面包：我吃，我领会。
到后来就是，我领会，我吃。
我房屋/身体/躯壳上的标记是
非洲武士身上
瘢痕的记忆：伤疤
被沉着地刻上，作为身份的象征。
我阅读它们就好像盲文。

他们找到我时我满身污垢，
粗野而谙哑。他们问我：发生了
什么事？同情打开了
记忆的笼子，话语从我倾泻而出
就好像格蕾特扔在黑森林里的面包屑，①
希望的小石子，
话语
变成了光
指给我
回家的路。

现在我被治好了。
但我再也不
像从前那样看。

（周伟驰　译）

----

① 格蕾特是格林童话《汉赛尔和格蕾特》的小姑娘，狠心的继母
两次把她和她哥哥抛弃在黑森林里，但兄妹俩凭着一路上扔小石子
和面包屑而找到了回家的路。译注。

Pronouncement

Chirikuré Chirikuré

the old woman sat
like a lone tree in a desert

slowly, gently
going over it again and again:
why her children?
why? why?

then she sighed, gravely
pronouncing, like a prophet:
if this revolution devours some children
not all
then some mothers will choose not to bear any

宣告

[津巴布韦] 齐里克热·齐里克热

年迈的妇人坐着
像沙漠中一棵孤零零的树

缓慢地，轻轻地
重复一遍又一遍：
为什么是她的孩子？
为什么？为什么？

然后她做了个手势，像一个
先知，沉重地宣告：
如果这革命吞噬了一些孩子
而不是全部
那么一些母亲将决定，不再有任何生育

（成婴　译）

Lament

Hama Tuma

Stillborn passions in decayed hearts
the tam tam is heard only by the deaf
scratched moons mock at broken souls
the sun is bent to burn its own shadow.
In the pond the frogs croak silently
the crocodile sleeps on the swan
 out in the field the bees gather cow dung
and the beetle reigns in the honeycombs.
Up by the mountain the heroes die
and the valley roars with the laughter
of cowards.
Tears are red and
flow back into dry eyes.
The mother refuses to bury her child
as piles of corpses are set alight.
The night continues and the day
flees back. No light is seen,
ideals have dried up:
Have the brave given up?

哀悼

[埃塞俄比亚] 哈玛·图玛

夭折的激情在腐烂的心里
咚咚声只被聋子听见
划伤的月亮嘲笑着破碎的灵魂
太阳被迫燃烧自己的影子。
在池塘中青蛙默默地呱呱叫
鳄鱼睡在天鹅上面
田野内外蜜蜂聚集在牛粪上
而甲虫统治着蜂巢。
在山上英雄们死去
山谷随着胆小鬼的笑声
吼叫。
泪水是红色的并且
流回到干涩的眼中。
母亲拒绝埋葬她的孩子
当成堆的尸体被点燃。
夜晚延续着而白天
逃了回去。看不到灯光,
理想干涸了:
勇敢已经被放弃?

(张曙光 译)

gone

Nii Ayikwei Parkes

> *"A bitter cold wind swept round them, and*
> *she felt something pulling at her dress. 'Quick,*
> *quick,' cried the Ghost"* – Oscar Wilde, The
> Canterville Ghost

before i can speak you're already gone
all of you, ghosts shimmering in the flames
of absence. i question you and the wind
answers. i am left with the spite of night.

the elders say you can only tell a frog's true length
when it dies; your bodies are now sand and bone,
no rulers can lay their digits on you.
i question you and the wind answers.

sarah, emma, jerry… – i could name you all;
you said crying was good, but you didn't say
which eye should first shed its load. this riddle
ages me. i question you and the wind answers.

yesterday i saw a dead frog, lonely
by the side of a road. i could tell
its length, but its voice had faded in the sun,
its green and blood were fused into mystery.

消逝

[加纳] 奈伊·阿伊克维·帕克斯

> "一阵冷风刺骨袭来,她感到有东西在拉
> 她的裙子,'快点,快点'鬼魂叫着"
>
> ——奥斯卡·王尔德《坎特维尔的幽灵》

在我开口之前你已消逝
全部的你,在缺席的火焰中
鬼魂闪烁。我问你
风却答话。我带着夜的怨恨离开

老话说,青蛙死后才知道
它到底多长,你已化为沙
变成骨,任何强力不能染指
我问你,风却答话。

萨拉,爱玛,杰瑞……我可以随便叫你
你说哭是好的,但没有说泪水
该从哪只眼里先落下。这个难题
让我变老。我问你,风却答话。

昨天,我看见一只死青蛙
独自躺在路边,我可以说出
它有多长,但日光中已消歇了蛙音
它的绿色和血也混入神秘

i turned to point out to you, but before
i could speak the wind blew my scarf away.

我转身指给你看，不及开口
风吹走了我的头巾。

（姜涛　译）

Worn

Joyce Chigiya

The trip to low lying Runde river (altitude five seventy)
I take sitting on the reed mat next to the hearth, a mbira in my hand
Depressions on the cool moss, moulds of my cracked feet
Stamping History that fades before circulation, where
elephants from the Trans-Frontier Park, forms against the dawn sky,
wash off my muddled yesterday, for the slate to be reusable.

磨损

[津巴布韦] 乔伊斯·齐基娅

润德河^①低伏（海拔五十七米）
去那儿的路上，我手拿蒙比拉琴^②
坐在炉边的苇席上。
地面阴冷潮湿，我双脚骨伤未愈
尘封的历史尚未流传就已褪色
那来自边境公园的大象，正列队在黄昏的天空下
为着往事重临，洗刷我泥泞的昨日

（姜涛　译）

---

① 流经津巴布韦东南部的一条河流。译注。
② 一种非洲的手指钢琴。译注。

The Mediterranean at Five

Stanley Onjezani Kenani

Like a baby asleep
The sea is calm at five
The water and all in it alive
Except the hungry souls swimming across
Prizing themselves from the jaws of poverty
To hungrier lions that maul them

These twittering five o'clock birds are deceptive
Even the innocence of the sleepy Mediterranean is not true
There are jaws within
Crocodiles that swallow our run-away brothers.

五点钟的地中海

[马拉维] 斯坦利·昂热扎尼·克那尼

像熟睡的婴儿
五点钟的大海平静无风
除了饥饿的灵魂
珍视自己从贫困的咽喉游向
更饥饿的狮子，撕裂自己的皮肉
海水和它的内部都蕴藏着生机

这些五点钟鸣啭的鸟是骗人的
甚至熟睡中不省人事的地中海也不真实
那些鳄鱼张开
鬼门关的咽喉吞下了我们逃难的兄弟。

（张伟栋　译）

The coca cola generation

Tjawangwa Dema

I've found me a new generation that dances to a different beat
Where all types of nations live on the same street
Red, white, black, colour and creed mean nothing
We as bubbly as soda in tin cans
Wrapped in a metallic world where colour has no credence

Go on grandma don't say a word
We don't want your tales of old woe
We weren't there we don't have to know
How they whipped your back senseless
Tearing skin, bloodying dress
Yet I see you still don't understand why we want no part of
this mess
Who needs the right idea
We found a working idea
When it hurts too much
We're made of tough stuff
We sit sipping Coca cola
On the phone screaming holler
Telling everyone we know
How much we don't know
Know what I mean

可口可乐一代①

[博茨瓦纳] 贾旺娃·迪玛

我发觉自己是新一代跳舞有不同的节拍
在那儿各个民族生活在同一条街上
红、白、黑、颜色和教条都无所谓
我们泡沫直冒像苏打水在锡罐里
被包装在一个金属的世界里在那儿颜色没什么信用

快走吧老奶奶不要说一句话
我们不想听你悲悲切切的老故事
故事发生时我们不在现场我们不必非得知道
他们怎样把你的后背鞭打得失去知觉
撕裂着的皮肤，流着血的衣服
不过我看你还是不懂为什么我们不想听你这乱糟糟的事
谁还要正确的观点
我们找到了管用的观点
当伤害来得太多
我们就硬起心肠
我们坐着把可口可乐啜饮
在电话里大声胡扯些什么
告诉我们认识的每一个人
我们什么也不知道
你知道吧

（周伟驰　译）

---

① 这首诗写年轻一代不爱听老一代的教诲，而以金属（汽车等物质）为人生目标，以喝可口可乐及打无聊电话逃避艰辛。诗中"胡扯些什么"是美国俚语，"你知道吧"是饶舌乐中的常用语。译注。

The Chelwood Papers

Tolu Ogunlesi

I
pussy cat, pussy cat
where else have you been?

to Birmingham to stew the Queen
in questions black-hot 'n spicy.

clutching a ticket that costs too much,
on a train whose doors throw tantrums

in an accent I nod to without hearing,
and without saying 'come again',

or 'pardon me'.
perhaps without even listening.

I will not ask you to listen to me either,
not now, not ever.

but I will ask for your weak sun, your safe passage,
your discounts, and your broadband.

II
The past is a foreign country.
So is the present.

切尔伍德书信集

[尼日利亚] 陶鲁·欧冈勒斯

I
小猫咪，小猫咪
你还去过哪里？

去伯明翰用黑辣香的
问题炖皇后？

抓紧一张太贵的票，
坐上车门喷怒气的火车。

我带有口音，
不曾听懂，不曾说"再来一遍"

或"请原谅"，甚至
连听都没注意听就点起头。

我也不会要你听我说，
现在不要，永远不要。

但我会要你虚弱的太阳，安全的人行道，
你的贴现率，还有你的宽频带。

II
过去是一个外国，
现在也是。

I am a citizen of the Future
but my passport's in processing.

this poem (mobile bus-stop
between song and language)

is my transit visa, homeless
like me, speaking a foreign language

like me. together we will enslave
this language, like they enslaved us;

the vowel as victim, the consonant
in dissonance.

III
I am a translated man, learning
the art of translation, that I might cast

a cold, unforgiving eye
on these pages I inhabit.

every time my pen stumbles, it will draw
blood. We will pretend it is ink.

which is thicker, it's hard to tell,
and both clot, in case you didn't know.

我是未来的公民，
可我的护照正在申办中。

这首诗（在歌曲和语言之间的
流动汽车站）

是我的过境签证，像我一样
无家可归，像我一样说着外语。

我们将一起奴役这种语言，
就像他们奴役我们；

元音好像牺牲品，
那不和谐的辅音韵。

III
我是一个被翻译的人，学习
翻译技巧，向我

栖居的这些页面
投去无情的白眼。

每次我的笔绊倒，它都会
流血，我们假装那是墨水。

很难说，哪样更浓，
两者都会凝结，假如你不知道。

IV
(for S.)

this language is not yours
but don't let that get to you.

language is not a bank account,
on which we earn interest

even if they sometimes want us to think so;
that there are hidden charges to be incurred

for not weaving your tongue like theirs.
take this land like an unsalted burger –

both with welcoming
arms, and a pinch of salt.

you will learn, and leave;
and learn to leave your money,

and parts of your tongue,
behind. Believe me.

IV

（给S.）

这种语言不是你的，
但不要让它收买你。

语言不是我们能从中
赚取利息的银行户头，

即使他们有时想让我们这么以为。
如果你没能像他们那样织舌头，

就会发生一些隐蔽的费用。
把这块土地当作没加盐的汉堡——

两者都有欢迎的
手臂和一小撮盐。

你将学习，然后离开，
并学会留下你的钱，

还要在身后留下
你的一部分舌头，相信我。

（丁丽英　译）

Maybe, Maybe Not

Keagometsi Joseph Molapong

Maybe my love will come, maybe not
I might lay my eyes on her beauty, yet I might not
Maybe there is a second dream, maybe not
Possibly a better dream of love, only possible
Maybe is such a confusing word, maybe

    Maybe I will be surprised one day, maybe
    I might hold her in my arms, yet I might not
    Maybe a vision will come to me, maybe not
    Possibly she will think of me, only possible
    Maybe is such an indefinite word, maybe.

Maybe the sun will rise tomorrow, maybe not
I might make sweet love to her, yet I might not
Maybe the truth will be revealed, maybe not
Possibly she will inherit my surname, only possibly
Maybe has so much meaning in it, maybe

    Maybe the night will be alive forever, maybe
    I might not be the one for her, yet I might
    Maybe I will wake up from my slumber, maybe not
    Possible, she loves her man, that man, possibly not
    Maybe, I possibly might not be, the one for her.

Maybe I am dreaming, maybe not

也许，也许不

［纳米比亚］齐莫格茨·约瑟夫·莫拉庞

也许我的爱将会到来，也许不会
我可能将眼睛寄放在她的美上，也许我不能
也许有第二个梦，也许没有
可能有一个更好的爱之梦，只是可能
也许是如此惑人的一个词，也许

　　也许有一天我会吃惊，也许
　　我能把她拥在怀，但也许我不能
　　也许我将具有远见，也许没有
　　可能她将想起我，只是可能
　　也许是如此无限的一个词，也许。

也许太阳将在明天升起，也许不
我能和她轻怜密爱，也许我不能
也许真实将被揭示，也许不会
可能她将继承我的姓氏，只是可能
也许的里面有太多意思，也许

　　也许夜晚将永远活着，也许
　　我可能不适合她，但或许我适合
　　也许我将从沉睡中醒来，也许不会
　　可能，她爱她的那个男人，也可能不爱
　　也许，我或许不可能是，她的良配。

也许我在做梦，也许不是

Maybe I am confused maybe not
There might be an answer,
There might be a possibility
There might be a chance
I might possibly be confused
Maybe by the word maybe

也许我迷惑了，也许不是
或许有一个答案
或许有一种可能
或许有一次机会
可能我被迷惑了
也许是被也许这个词

（杨铁军　译）

I like pain

Beaven Tapureta

I like pain
I am its child
I like sorrow
I am its father
I like
Struggle, it will set me free!

我喜欢痛苦

［津巴布韦］比温·塔普莱塔

我喜欢痛苦
我是它的孩子
我喜欢悲伤
我是它的父亲
我喜欢
斗争，它将让我自由！

（韩博　译）

My spirit Mother

Ama Ata Aidoo

My spirit Mother ought to come for me earlier.
Now what shall I tell them who are gone? The daughter of

Slaves who come from the white man's land.
Someone should advise me on how to tell my story
my children, I am dreading my arrival there
where they will ask me news of home.
Shall I tell them or shall I not?
Someone should lend me a tongue
Light enough with which to tell
My Royal Dead
That one of their stock
Has gone away and brought to their sacred precincts
The wayfarer!

They will ask me where I was
when such things were happening.
Oh mighty God!
Even when the Unmentionable
Came and carried off the children of the house
in shoals like fish

我的老祖宗[①]

［加纳］阿玛·阿塔·艾杜

我的老祖宗早该保佑我。
如今，怎么向他们的在天之灵交代？这闺女

是白人地界的奴隶后裔。
谁能指点我如何讲述我的故事
孩子们，我很怕死后见到祖宗
他们会盘问我家里的事情
我该说，还是不该说？
谁又能借我一条巧舌
轻松地打发我尊贵的祖宗
告诉他们
流着他们血脉的一个儿孙从远方归来
为他们的圣土带回了
一个孤魂野鬼！

他们会盘问我，
当初我在哪儿。
哦，老天爷！
当那个我不愿再提起的人
带走家里的孩子
就像捡走浅滩上的鱼儿

---

① 此诗出自于Aidoo的第一本剧本《The Dilemma of a Ghost》。加
纳留美学生Ato学成携妻美国黑人Eulalie返乡。当家人得知其妻为黑
奴之后不禁大吃一惊。译注。

Nana Kum kept his feet steadfast on the ground
And refused to let any of his nephews
take a wife from a doubtful stock.

库姆老祖母撩出双脚摆出架式
决不让家里的子侄
从不清不白的种里捡媳妇

（黄景路　译）

After the Deluge

Wole Soyinka

Once, for a dare,
He filled his heart-shaped swimming pool
With bank notes, high denomination
And fed a pound of caviar to his dog.
The dog was sick; a chartered plane
Flew in replacement for the Persian rug.

He made a billion yen
Leap from Tokyo to Buenos Aires,
Turn somersaults through Brussels,
New York, Sofia and Johannesburg.
It cracked the bullion market open wide.
Governments fell, coalitions cracked
Insurrection raised its bloody flag
From north to south.

He knew his native land through iron gates,
His sight was radar bowls, his hearing
Electronic beams. For flesh and blood,
Kept company with a brace of Dobermanns.
But - yes - the worthy causes never lacked
His widow's mite, discreetly publicised.

He escaped the lynch days. He survives.
I dreamt I saw him on a village

洪荒之后

［尼日利亚］沃莱·索因卡

一度，明明知道危险，
他用自己的心形泳池
来装银行支票，都是大面额
还给自己的狗喂了一磅鱼子酱。
狗病了；一架包机
代替波斯飞毯飞来飞去。

他挣了十亿日元
从东京跃向布宜诺斯艾利斯，
在布鲁塞尔，纽约，索非亚
和约翰内斯堡之间连翻筋斗。
这让黄金市场剧烈震荡。
政府垮台，同盟破裂
从南到北
到处揭竿而起，红旗翻卷。

他关紧大门来了解祖国，
他的眼力是雷达槽，听力是
电子束。至于肉身，
则与一对杜宾犬形影不离。
不过——没错——高尚事业也从
少不了他略尽绵薄，这些都谦谨地加以宣传。

他逃脱了私刑算账的日子。他保住了命。
我曾梦见在一个村子的输水管线上

Water line, a parched land where
Water is a god
That doles its favours by the drop,
And waiting is a way of life.
Rebellion gleamed yet faintly in his eye
Traversing chrome-and-platinum retreats. There,
Hubs of commerce smoothly turn without
His bidding, and cities where he lately roosted
Have forgotten him, the preying bird
Of passage.

They let him live, but not from pity
Or human sufferance. He scratches life
From earth, no worse a mortal man than the rest.
Far, far away in dreamland splendour,
Creepers twine his gates of bronze relief.
The jade-lined pool is home
To snakes and lizards; they hunt and mate
On crusted algae.

看见了他，那是块炎热的土地
水就是上帝
论滴来行它的恩惠，
而等待就是一种生活方式。
他的眼中闪着反抗但已微弱
一种脱胎换骨的引退。在那儿，
商业中心没有他的买卖
也运行顺畅，他新近栖身的城市
已经忘掉他，这迁徙的
掠食猛禽。

他们让他活着，但非出于同情
也不是人类的容忍。他在尘世中
拼命，终有一死，不比他人强到哪里。
遥远的，在远在天边的梦境般的光辉中，
葡萄藤缠绕着他青铜浮雕的大门。
绿玉砌边的游泳池
是蛇和蜥蜴之家；他们追逐着，交配着
在皮老壳硬的海藻里。

（席亚兵　译）

I sigh for home

Joyce Chigiya

Smoke that drifts over graying thatch like it would
from grandfather's pipe, dissipates into wintry air.
Dust wafts in khaki clouds as a head-scarfed maid
rearranges sand particles ridding them of white-patch-on
black fowl droppings and leaves strewn all over the yard.
    (Heave) The sights of home.

The ear picks from the kraal a moo so low it can hardly
shake a feather, as the sole survivor of the drought
yearns for reunification with departed mates and offspring.
The cockrel springs off to perch upon the hollow grainery stores
to announce, "A brand new day begins!"(soh la la la me ray doh)
    (Heave) The sounds of home

From the kitchen hut, the odour of the mopani tree,
that forthcoming fuel, clings onto the smoke to float along.
Burning meal cuts in as the finger millet porridge erupts
from the claypot like lava, to fill the hearth with chocolate
killing the fire on impact, reducing the wood to black stumps.
    (Heave) The smells of home.

In the evenings we sit around fires where stories are heard and told,

为家叹息

[津巴布韦] 乔伊斯·齐基娅

烟从花白的茅草上升起，就像从
祖父的烟斗里冒出，消散在寒风中。
浓烟中的尘埃，如一个围了头巾的女仆
收起沙粒，又将它们洒向芦花鸡背
鸡粪和落叶覆盖着场院
　　（长叹一声）：家的景象。

牛栏里探出的耳朵，哞哞的叫声低沉得甚至
不能撼动羽毛，像大旱中唯一的幸存者
渴望与亲人重逢，渴望清泉
斗鸡暴起高踞在空空的谷仓之上
宣称，"新的一天开始了"（嗦啦啦啦秘来哆）
　　（长叹一声）：家的声音

厨棚里，柴薪不愁，莫帕尼树①
的芳香，混合了浓烟飘散
当食物在火上焦糊，米粥突然像熔岩
从罐子里冒出，巧克力汁满溢了炉膛
一下子浇灭了火焰，木柴变成乌黑的残骸
　　（长叹一声）：家的味道

许多夜晚，我们坐在火边，说长道短

---

① 莫帕尼树，具有蝴蝶形叶子的树种，广泛分布在南非、博茨瓦纳、纳米比亚等地。译注。

of Hyena's greed, of Rabbit's treachery, of heroes, heroines and villains. I have been to Jo'burg without crossing the Limpopo, seen the gold get into my eyes just like the sun, all this through the eye in my core, though. And yet everytime I think of home, I sigh.

海耶纳的贪婪，拉比特的背叛，男女英雄和坏蛋
未经林波波^①，我到过约翰内斯堡，如同见到太阳
亲眼见过黄金，尽管这一切，都被我的内在之眼看透
但每一次想到家，我还是叹息。

（姜涛　译）

---

① Limpopo，南非最北边的省份。译注。

IV Love

In all its diversity, love engages and challenges the soul to be better, to be kinder, to be stronger. In these poems that capture relationships with family, lovers and dreams, we follow the poet's maps to the human heart, over the broken glass of deceit and betrayal, cynicism and boredom. The poet's vision moves over different landscapes in its attempt to capture and reflect the places where she or he hopes to fully realize the self, without limitation. But this is a rare place, easily lost or overlooked. The poets chart the place where the poet becomes aware of the fragility of being and the unutterable immensity of the gift of love.

IV 爱

在扑朔迷离之中，爱介入并激励着灵魂，使其更美好、更善良、更坚强。这些诗处理着与家庭、爱人及梦境的关联，诗人带领我们探入人类心灵，俯视破碎的幻境，其中的欺骗、背叛、讽刺与无聊暴露无遗。诗人的目光不受羁绊，扫过不同的领地，力图捕捉、呈现出她或他希望充分实现自我的地方。但是，此境绝少，易被遗失或忽略。诗人点化出人性脆弱之处以及言不可喻的深情厚意。

The eyes of the one I know

Keagometsi Joseph Molapong

Her eyes talk of sincerity
And explain the inside
Of the person it looks at
They search, tease, invite
The inside into the open

我认识的那人的眼睛

［纳米比亚］齐莫格茨·约瑟夫·莫拉庞

她的眼诉说着真诚
解释了它所观看的
那人的内心
它们搜寻，挑逗，邀请
内心到开放之处

（杨铁军　译）

song of the mundane

Shabbir Banoobhai

sprouting in the ears of corn
running down the noses of leaves
drooling from the mouths of flowers

this too is love

the cataracts in the eyes of age
the wrinkled skin of wisdom
the dry white hair of time

this too is love

multiplying the fruit
instead of dividing the land
adding care, subtracting hate

this too is love

noticing the darkness of the sun
or the light that breaks open
from a new-born wound

this too is love

mending a fragile thought

尘世之歌

［南非］沙比尔·巴努海

谷粒的耳朵萌芽
树叶的鼻子流涕
花朵的嘴巴垂涎

这也是爱

年龄眼中的奔流
智慧皮肤的褶皱
时间干枯的白发

这也是爱

增殖水果
别去分裂土地
增加关爱，减少憎恨

这也是爱

注意太阳的黑暗
或一处新伤口
破开的光线

这也是爱

缝补易碎的思想

rebuilding hope from despair
washing dishes with one's hands

this too is love

the pebble thrown into a stream
with no hope of being retrieved
free to unburden its hardness

this too is love

meticulously arranging words
into a net to catch the early light
before it solidifies and is drowned

this too is love

picking up the litter when the work
for the day is done so that night
will not need to hide it

this too is love

重建绝望后的希望
亲手清洗碗碟

这也是爱

掷于溪流的卵石
不再复归原处
不再负坚固之担

这也是爱

精心安排的词句
在僵化且溺毙之前
编织成网以捕捉曙光

这也是爱

一日工作已尽
拾捡垃圾
以便夜晚不必将它藏匿

这也是爱

（韩博　译）

Speaking of hearts

Makhosazana Xaba

It is hard to drag a painful heart everywhere she goes.
So, she packs it in a drawer where she keeps her underwear
to comfort it with the warmth of intimacy. Then
goes out with a friend; watch a movie, have dinner.
When her friend asks: how is your heart?
She answers: resting, awash with memories.

说说心脏

[南非] 马克霍萨萨纳·萨巴

她感觉拖一颗疼痛的心脏到处跑太累。
所以，她把它装入一个放满内衣的抽屉
用轻柔的温暖宽慰它。然后
与朋友一同出去：看电影，吃饭。
朋友问她：你的心脏怎么样了？
她回答："休息着，浸入记忆之水。

（叶美　译）

Thirty pieces

Tjawangwa Dema

How much silver would it take
For you to walk a little slower
On a day when right summons haste
How much silver would it take
For you to turn the other cheek
To not heed what needs to be seen
How much silver would it take
For you to give up yourself
Give up a moment of your peace
For someone else

三十块①

［博茨瓦纳］贾旺娃·迪玛

你会要多少钱
才会走得慢一点
当某天某事需要你快一点
你会要多少钱
才会转过另一边脸
对该管的事掉头不看
你会要多少钱
才会放弃你自己
放弃你一刻的心安
为了别人

（周伟驰　译）

---

① "三十块"系指犹大为了三十块钱出卖了耶稣。译注。

when love seeks, it becomes a lover

Shabbir Banoobhai

when love seeks, it becomes a lover
when love finds, it becomes the beloved

when love seeks, it becomes an illness
when love finds, it becomes a cure

when love seeks, it becomes a door
when love finds, it becomes a key

when love seeks, it becomes a book
when love finds, it becomes meaning

when love seeks, it becomes a lover
when love finds, it becomes the beloved

when love seeks, it becomes beauty
when love finds, it becomes truth

when love seeks, it becomes a messenger
when love finds, it becomes the message

when love seeks, it becomes a sea
when love finds, it becomes a ship

when love seeks, it becomes a lover

当爱寻觅，它便是爱人

［南非］沙比尔·巴努海

当爱寻觅，它便是爱人
当爱寻获，它便是所爱

当爱寻觅，它便是疾病
当爱寻获，它便是治愈

当爱寻觅，它便是大门
当爱寻获，它便是钥匙

当爱寻觅，它便是书籍
当爱寻获，它便是意义

当爱寻觅，它便是爱人
当爱寻获，它便是所爱

当爱寻觅，它便是美貌
当爱寻获，它便是真理

当爱寻觅，它便是信使
当爱寻获，它便是信息

当爱寻觅，它便是大海
当爱寻获，它便是船只

当爱寻觅，它便是爱人

when love finds, it becomes the beloved

when love seeks, it becomes a seed
when love finds, it becomes fruit

when love seeks, it becomes a branch
when love finds, it becomes shade

when love seeks, it becomes thirst
when love finds, it becomes a drink

when love seeks, it becomes a lover
when love finds, it becomes the beloved

when love seeks, it becomes earth
when love finds, it becomes the sky

when love seeks, it becomes a cloud
when love finds, it becomes rain

when love seeks, it becomes a storm
when love finds, it becomes calm

when love seeks, it becomes a lover
when love finds, it becomes the beloved

when love seeks, it becomes movement
when love finds, it becomes stillness

当爱寻获，它便是所爱

当爱寻觅，它便是种子
当爱寻获，它便是果实

当爱寻觅，它便是枝条
当爱寻获，它便是树荫

当爱寻觅，它便是干渴
当爱寻获，它便是啜饮

当爱寻觅，它便是爱人
当爱寻获，它便是所爱

当爱寻觅，它便是大地
当爱寻获，它便是天空

当爱寻觅，它便是云朵
当爱寻获，它便是雨水

当爱寻觅，它便是暴风
当爱寻获，它便是宁静

当爱寻觅，它便是爱人
当爱寻获，它便是所爱

当爱寻觅，它便是运动
当爱寻获，它便是歇止

when love seeks, it becomes speech
when love finds, it becomes silence

when love seeks, it becomes generosity
when love finds, it becomes gratitude

when love seeks, it becomes a lover
when love finds, it becomes the beloved

when love seeks, it becomes humility
when love finds, it becomes grace

when love seeks, it becomes absence
when love finds, it becomes presence

when love seeks, it becomes dark
when love finds, it becomes light

when love seeks, it becomes a lover
when love finds, it becomes the beloved

当爱寻觅，它便是言说
当爱寻获，它便是无语

当爱寻觅，它便是慷慨
当爱寻获，它便是感恩

当爱寻觅，它便是爱人
当爱寻获，它便是所爱

当爱寻觅，它便是谦恭
当爱寻获，它便是优雅

当爱寻觅，它便是缺席
当爱寻获，它便是即席

我爱寻觅，它便是黑暗
当爱寻获，它便是光明

当爱寻觅，它便是爱人
当爱寻获，它便是所爱

（韩博　译）

Letter from Havana
(for Baby K)

Keorapetse Kgositsile

A while back I said
with my little hand upon
the tapestry of memory and my loin
leaning on the blues to find voice:
If loving you is wrong
I do not want to do right

Now though I do not possess
A thousand thundering voices
like Mazisi kaMdabuli weKunene
nor Chris Abani's mischievous courage
as I trace the shape of desire and longing
I wish I was a cartographer of dreams
but what I end up with is this stubborn question:
Should I love my heart more
because every time I miss you
that is where I find you

寄自哈瓦那
（给宝贝K）

[南非] 凯奥拉佩策·考斯尔

刚才，我的小手
抚摸着记忆的壁毯
腰倚着布鲁斯，寻找着
语言，我说：
如果爱你是错的
我不想做对

现在，虽然我没有
马·卡·韦库尼尼①那样
雷鸣般恢宏的嗓音
也没有克里斯·阿巴尼②顽皮的勇气
当我追踪欲望和渴求的形状
我希望我是一个梦的绘图师
而我终止于这个执拗的问题：
我应更爱我的心吗
因为每当我想念你
我就能在它那里找到你

（冷霜　译）

---

① 马·卡·韦库尼尼（1930—2006），南非第一任国家桂冠诗
人，也是作者的挚友。译注。
② 克里斯·阿巴尼（1966—　），尼日利亚作家、诗人，曾因其
小说和戏剧作品多次入狱，现居美国。译注。

العمياء

فاطمة ناعوت

التي أبصرتْ فجأةً
بعد جراحةٍ مرتبكةٍ تمَّتْ على عجلٍ
يناسبُ ارتكابَ الشِّعرِ
في صورتِهِ المحرَّمةُ.

عهدٌ طويلٌ مع الشخوصِ إلى الأعلى
بأحداقٍ فارغة،
سمعتُ خلالها عشراتِ الكُتبِ
لكنَّها
حين راقصتْ "لاما"
عندَ سَفْحِ الهضبةِ،
علَّمها أن صعودَ الرُّوحِ
مرهونٌ بانفصالِها الشَّبكيِّ.

أُميَّةٌ إذن
لأن الألمَ المرسومَ على ملامحِها
لحظةَ الإعلاءِ الجسديّ
أفسدَ النصَّ
فانثنى القلمُ
قبل اكتمالِ الحكاية.

لا سبيلَ للرجوع الآن
المعرفةُ في اتِّجاهِها
والجهلُ
فردوسٌ غائب.

盲女

[埃及] 法蒂玛·纳乌特

她突见光明
伴随复杂手术的迅速完成
犹如犯罪般的痛苦
恰能激起人们赋诗的泉涌。

很久以来
她那无神的双目
仰望天空,
聆听过数十本书声
但在山脚下,
当她和"喇嘛"起舞
他教化她灵魂能脱俗超升
如不在视网膜的束缚之中。

由于无知
她满面愁容
恍惚中
撕坏了课本
折断了笔
故事仍在进行中。

现在随着知识的到来
已无路可退
无知
是逝者的乐园。

لذا
تظلُّ الفكرةُ تُطِلُّ برأسِها
محضَ ذاكرةٍ جافةٍ
كلما راودَها البصرُ .
تسكبُ ظلَّينِ واقفينْ
في عتمةِ ردهةٍ مبهورةِ الأنفاسِ
صامتةٌ
كانت تستعدُّ للشاي
عند انتهاءِ المشهدْ .

ظلَّانِ
أحدُهما يمارسُ مهنةَ التنويرِ
والآخرُ
يجتهدُ أن يقرأ
لكن
تَحُولُ دهشتُهُ العميقةُ
دون اكتمالِ الدرسِ.

القراءةُ لا تحتاجُ إلى عينين
هذا ما تأكَّد لها
حين أبصرتْ فجأةً
ولم تجدْ كتابًا .

274

但是
那些枯竭的记忆
一直萦绕不散
每当她睁开双眼。
仿佛有两个影子站在身边
在暗淡、令人窒息
寂静的客厅里
她备好了茶点，
正当节目的最后。

两个影子，
一个是灯光技师
另一个
忙着阅读，
但是
未完成课程
令人震惊。

无庸置疑
阅读无需眼睛
当她突见光明
却发现无书可读。

（刘炼，刘宝莱　译）

Jailbirds

Amanda Hammar

Our footsteps heavy against
the granite surface of our days.
Your callous/ed fingers
careless across my ribs.

Abrasions of the ordinary.

Our bed a prison now,
a shared stretch
of solitary confinement.
Our proximity a lie.

囚犯

［津巴布韦］阿曼达·哈玛

我们的脚步沉重地敲打
日子的花岗石表面。
你们结茧（无情）的手指
粗率地绕过我的肋骨。

普通的擦伤。

现在我们的床是一所
分享
单独监禁时光的监狱。
我们的接近是谎言。

（张伟栋　译）

Silence

Stanley Onjezani Kenani

We lie apart. Sweating. Spent. Breathing like athletes on the finishing line. An owl hoots outside. Strange sound at lunch hour. You fart. I rush to open the window; clean air to cleanse our souls. You lie still. Silence. Maybe death is like that: so sweet, then silence.

What would my wife say, seeing me naked like this? Next to a woman equally undressed? "My husband is in America," you say. You do not explain why. "My wife . . ." my voice dies. I am saved by the hooting owl. Silence. Maybe death is like that: many unfinished sentences, then silence.

I grab the remote control on the bedside. I switch on the telly. A commercial on AIDS. "Abstain . . . Protected Sex . . . blah, blah, blah" You snatch the remote. Switch off. "Life's too short," you say. "Pessimism makes it shorter." Kisses. Silence. Maybe death is like that: pessimism, kisses, then silence.

You sleep. Snore. Talk in your sleep. "I love you, my husband!" you say. "With all my heart. With all my soul." I remember my own lies. The birthday cake I bought my wife yesterday. "With all my love," inscribed prominently on it. "I love my wife too," I say out loud. Silence. Maybe death is like that: lies, then silence.

沉默

[马拉维] 斯坦利·昂热扎尼·克那尼

我们分开躺着。渗着汗。虚度着。呼吸像终点线的
运动员。外面猫头鹰哀嚎。这午餐时光奇怪的声
响。你放了屁。我冲过去开窗；干净的空气清洗了
我们的灵魂。你仍躺着。无言。也许死亡就是如
此；这样甜蜜，然后沉默。

看到我这样裸露着，又挨着你这个赤裸的女人，我
的妻子会怎样想呢？"我的丈夫在美国。"你说。
你没有再说下去。"我妻子……"我的声音漠然。
猫头鹰的哀嚎为了解围。沉默。也许死亡就是如
此；没说几句，然后沉默。

我抓起床旁的遥控器。打开电视。艾滋病广告。
"禁欲……防护的性交……胡扯，废话，脑屎"你
夺走遥控器。关掉。"生命是短暂的，"你说。"悲
观的生命更短暂。"亲吻。沉默。也许死亡就是如
此：悲观，亲吻，然后沉默。

你睡去。打鼾。梦里低语。"我爱你，丈夫！"你
说。"真心真意。"我记起了自己的谎言。昨天我买
给妻子的生日蛋糕。刻着显眼的字"全心爱你"。
"我也爱我的妻子，"我大声喊出。沉默。也许死亡
就是如此：谎言，然后沉默。

（张伟栋　译）

A-mar-me-te

Tânia Tomé

Abril esconde-nos
nas sinuosas curvas
das palavras.

Desabrocha
uma falésia
na embriaguez
do meu canto.

Aí se turva a linha
no instante
em que estamos
dentro
um do outro
dentro.

我爱你

[莫桑比克] 塔尼娅·托麦

四月，我们隐藏在
词语间的
逶迤曲折中

内心沉醉
花儿在幻境中
绽放

线条失去色彩
那一刻
我们在彼此的心中。

（鲁扬　译）

RIO

Tânia Tomé

Me ancoraste
exactamente aqui
onde te rio.

Ri comigo
meu amor,
vê
como se amplia
o cais.

笑

[莫桑比克] 塔尼娅·托麦

让我靠岸吧
就在这里
我向你放声大笑。

跟我一起笑吧
我的爱人，
看
港湾越来越大。

（鲁扬　译）

ሕይወት

Alemu Tebeje Ayele

ባድማስ ግርግዳነት፤
ምድር ሆኖ ወለል፤
ሰማይ ደግሞ ጣራ፤
በመፈጠር ጥበብ፤
ይህች ዓለም ተዋቅራ፤
ተዋናዩ ፍጥረት፤
ይስተዋልባታል፤
ቴአትር ተሰርቶ፤
ቴአትር ሲሰራ።
ሁሉም የበኩሉን፤
በየድረሻው ሰርቶ፤
መኖርን ይኖራል፤
ወይ ሞቱን ይሞታል
ለሕይወት ሕይወት ሰጥቶ።
ቴአትር ነች ሕይወት፤
ዓለም ደግሞ ቤት፤
ህፃኑ ሲወለድ፤
የሚሞተው ሞቶ፤ እየቀጠዷት
ተዋናይ ታዳሚ፤
ታዳሚ ተዋናይ፤
ሆነው ተሁዋሁነው የሚኖሩባት።

284

生活

[埃塞俄比亚] 阿莱姆·特伯热·艾尔

地平线是墙
大地是地板
天空是屋顶
皆来自我们已成世界的
创作智慧
我们看到生物，有戏剧正在它身上上演
持续表演直到离开。
每一个已完成他被分配的角色
活着，再死掉自己
赋予他的存在以生命。
生命只是一次演出，世界只是一个家
当一个孩子出生，别的那么多人要死去
一直这么持续着。
演员是观众，观众是演员
一起生活在演出之中。

（成婴　译自英语）

Moonlight

Chirikuré Chirikuré

Let's dance the muchongoyo dance
Under the careful watch of the moon

Let's give the dance all our hearts
For the moon only comes but at night

Let's shake to the drums, sweating joyously
For, when the sun comes in the morning
It will take away the moon's soft, cool light
Crowning the day with blazing, golden arrows
Which tear apart the spirit that drives muchongoyo

月光

［津巴布韦］齐里克热·齐里克热

让我们跳姆冲戈尤舞①
在月亮小心的看护下

让我们全心全意地跳舞
因为月亮只在晚上来

让我们晃动手鼓，快乐地出汗
因为，当太阳伴晨曦而来
它将把月亮柔和的清辉带走
冠白日以炽热金色的箭矢
将射破驱动我们跳姆冲戈尤舞的精神

（成婴　译）

---

① 　姆冲戈尤舞是一种津巴布韦绍纳族的传统舞蹈。译注。

كراسة رسم

فاطمة ناعوت

عند الأربعين
تَكْبُرُ حقائبُ النساءِ
لتسعَ قُرصَ الضغطِ وقُمعَ السُّكرِ
ونظّارةً
تجعلُ الحَدقةَ أكبرَ
والحروفَ المراوغةَ
أكثرَ طِيبةً.

في الجيبِ السريّ
يضعنَ تذكرةَ داوود
ووصفةً ضدَّ غُصّةِ الحَلْقِ
التي تناوبُ كلّما مَحَقَ القمرْ،
وشمعةً
فالنارُ تحرِقُ العفاريتَ التي
تتسلّلُ في الليلْ
لتجزَّ أعناقَ الحريم،
وفي الجيبِ الأماميّ
وصيّةً:
لا أملكُ سوى آثارِ لونٍ
(عَلِقَ بكفي حين حطَّتْ عليها فراشتان)
وكراسة رسمٍ
وفرشاة،
أهبُها
-   شأنَ كلِّ موجودة-
للوطن.

写生簿

[埃及] 法蒂玛·纳乌特

人到四十
女士的手提包变大
内装降压药、糖块和
眼镜
增强视力
让模糊的字句
更为清晰。

在内衣口袋里
她们收藏着大卫的门票
以及防止打嗝的处方
每当月蚀，
点燃一枝蜡烛
犹如火焰烧死魔鬼
因为他们在夜间出没
割断女人的喉咙，
在外衣口袋里
装有一个愿望：
我只拥有"颜色的痕迹"
（当两只蝴蝶落在上面时它碰到了我的手臂）
一个写生簿
和一支画笔，
——犹如每一位孤独的女人——
我将它献给
祖国。

عند الأربعين
يتسرّبُ الصقيعُ إلى الجواربِ
ويغدو القلبُ صحنًا خاويًا،
لحظةَ هجرةِ الفراشاتِ من البيت
مساءَ الجمعة،
إلى أين تمضي الفراشات؟
تحطُّ على كَتَفِ العَمّة الطيّبة
في شرق العاصمة،
والسيدةُ الواجمةُ
تقبعُ في الشرفةِ
انتظارًا لموسم العودة
ليالِيَ سِتًّا.

وعند الأربعين
تقولُ المرأةُ لجارتِها
عندي صبيٌّ
لا يحبُّ الكلامَ،
والربُّ يُمهلُني
حتى ينطقَ ذاتِ وعدٍ:
يا أمُّ اذهبي!
أنا الآنَ
بخير.

人到四十
长袜透出白霜
心似盘碟变得空空荡荡，
当蝴蝶离家而去
在一个周五的晚上，
它们飞向何处？
原来落在一位善良阿姨的肩上
就在首都的东郊，
有六个晚上
那位沉默、悲伤的女士
坐在阳台上
等待它们归来。

人到四十
一位女士对她的邻居讲，
我有个儿子，
不爱说话，
愿真主给我时间
直到有一天早上
让他开口说：
妈妈，去吧！
我现在很好。

（刘炼，刘宝莱　译）

291

age is a beautiful phase

James Matthews

age is a beautiful phase
i am at peace with my journey
moving with contentment to its
end
where i will be at ease and
reflect upon the treasures gathered
sharing with those that have
none

age is not an omen of fear
terrifying in its presence
announcing the imminence of
death
it is the realization that
winter's sun has a vestige of
warmth that will pleasure my
days

age is a sanctuary that will
transform itself into an oasis
that is the terminus of my
travel
leaving me pleased to reflect
the years gathered have turned
into a pattern of periods of

老年是一个美丽的阶段

[南非] 詹姆斯·马修斯

老年是一个美丽的阶段
我对我的旅程心平气和
我移动着并满意于它的
终点
在那里我将感到安逸
分发聚集的财宝
跟那些一无所有的人
分享

老年并非恐惧的预兆
恐慌于它的出场
把死亡的紧迫
宣告
它乃是认识到
冬天的太阳尚有温暖的
痕迹它将令我的日子
愉悦

老年是一座圣所它将
把自己转变成一个绿洲
它是我旅行的
终点站
留下我快乐地反思
积攒的年份业已变成
时间的一种

time

age is an intoxicant that becomes
headier through the years with its
potency making me merry in my
sojourn
in each passageway savouring
the sweetness of my stay that shall
fortify me for the years forthcoming
age is a beautiful phase

分期模式

老年是一种致醉品变得愈来愈
醉人随着岁月的流逝以它的
威力使我沉醉于我的
旅居
在每一条通道都欣赏
我所驻之处的甜蜜它将
坚强我面对即将来临的岁月
老年是一个美丽的阶段

（周伟驰　译）

显像 4　胡项城

（Appearance IV　Hu Xiangcheng）

My name is *Gentle Fingers*

Makhosazana Xaba

When we woke up that morning
everyone had an errand to run,
it was the day of my sister's 50th birthday party.

I, with Mama almost alone in the house,
hoped she would focus on me
so she could call me by my name.

I persistently called her Mama
Wishing, hoping, dreaming, she might
call me by my name, at least once.

I walked her to the bathroom,
washed her, while she asked for directions
on what to do next.

Back in the bedroom
I used my body cream
on her dry and creased skin.

Then she looked me in the eye and smiled.
Without calling me by my name she said:
Yours are gentle fingers.

我的名字是*温柔的手指*

［南非］马克霍萨萨纳·萨巴

清晨我醒来
每个人都忙着自己的差事，
这天是姐姐50岁的生日会。

我，与母亲单独呆在房间，
希望她注意到我
这样她就会叫我的名字。

我热切地，满怀希望地，
一遍遍地喊妈妈，梦想她或许
叫我的名字，至少一次。

我们走入浴室，
她询问了下一步
该做些什么时，我给她洗澡。

卧室里
我用自己的沐浴露
擦她褶皱的干皮肤。

这次她定神看着我，微笑。
她开口却并未称呼我的名字：
你是温柔的手指。

（叶美　译）

My life

Hama Tuma

I sat by the rushing river
watching my life
slime and froth
clean and lost, pass by.
I heard its rugged dound
the jagged wail of of its solitude
saw its colourful charm
and the dark streak of despair
that covered it like welts.
I saw and heard my life
              as it rushed by
Ignoring me.

我的生命

［埃塞俄比亚］哈玛·图玛

我坐在奔流的河边
注视着我的生命
黏土和泡沫
洁净而迷惘，经过。
我听到它起伏的声音
它参差的孤独悲叹
看到它多彩的魅力
和绝望黑暗的线条
覆盖着它像鞭痕。
我看到并听见我的生命
　　　　当它奔流而过
对我毫不理睬。

（张曙光　译）

There is a me that I could be

Lebogang Mashile

There is a me that I could be
If I just let her breathe outside.
A thundering song that I could sing
If I just let her breathe outside.

There is a me who lives unseen
She paces the corridors inside
She's made of dreams that flow in between
These walls in my mind
She's my internal shadow traversing time
The relentless hope that slowly seeps through my eyes
Like the sun draped dawn,
She never asks why it is her job to ignite me,
Her purpose, to be my guide
To the me that I could be
If I just let her breathe outside
To the thundering song that I could sing
If I just let her breathe outside

Transformation is the spirit changing gear.
The elements of one's being becoming aware
That the future is always far
When your feet are firmly planted here
Attached to the present
Rooted in fear

有一个我本来可以成为的我

[南非] 勒布干·马希尔

有一个我本来可以成为的我
只要我让她到外面呼吸。
有一首我本来可以唱的响亮的歌
只要我让她到外面呼吸。

有一个看不见地生活着的我
她移步在内在的走廊里
她是由在我心里的这些高墙之间
流动着的梦儿构成
她是我内在的阴影纵贯着时间
她是不屈的希望慢慢地溢出我的双眼
像太阳悬挂在拂晓,
她从来不问为何点亮我是她的工作,
她的目的,是成为我的向导
导向我本可以成为的我
只要我让她到外面呼吸
导向我本可以唱的响亮的歌
只要我让她到外面呼吸

转变是精神在换挡。
一个人在生活中开始意识到
未来总是很遥远
当你的双脚被牢牢地栽种在这里
依附于现在
植根于恐惧

Change is the pulse of possibility

Pulling from the periphery to the now

It is the questions unanswered

The journey through the why's and the how's

It is a sojourn through darkness with a solitary flame as guide

It is the sole destination, the navigator and the ride

It is the blue light revelation revealed when morning cracks

It is abundance when you have known how it feels to live is lack

It is the race, the car, the ref, the scorecard and the track,

It is eyes fixed to the horizon with angels at your back

It is the purpose held with reverence reverted to when doubt attacks

It is an energizing uncertainty leaving no option of turning back

Always shifting

Always present

Demanding of us to be more than who we see ourselves to be

Than what we were before

Tomorrow is an infinite portal with no ceiling and no floor

There is only the ledge that beckons us

And wings designed for us to soar

There is a me that I could be

If I just let her breathe outside

A thundering song that I could sing

If I just let her breathe outside

There is a me who lives unseen

She paces the corridors inside

改变是可能性的脉动

从边缘拉到现在

它是未得到回答的问题

途经"为何"和"如何"的旅程

它是一次逗留途经黑暗以孤单的火焰为向导

它是唯一的目的地，领航员和骑马人

它是蓝光的启示在早晨破晓时被开启

它是富饶当你已知道"生活即缺乏"是什么感受

它是比赛、汽车、裁判员、记分卡和轨道，

它是双眼凝望着地平线而天使在你的身后

它是目的在受到怀疑攻击时被带着敬意地重提

它是精力充沛的不确定性不留下返回的余地

总是移动

总是现在

要求着我们高于我们以为自己所是的人

高于我们以前所是的人

明天是一个无边的入口既没有天花板也没有地板

唯有壁架召唤我们

唯有翅膀设计好了让我们翱翔

有一个我本来可以成为的我

只要我让她到外面呼吸

有一首我本来可以唱的响亮的歌

只要我让她到外面呼吸

有一个看不见地生活着的我

她移步在内在的走廊里

（周伟驰　译）

Constellation

Nii Ayikwei Parkes

In your father's house they dance on sand,
they turn their noses up at concrete
and when asked why they will speak
of the star-flecked night before you left:

Your father has thrown you a party
and you are dancing with the colourful
abandon and sweat of transition. Your
uncle – the peacekeeper who returned
from a tour of duty with a sturdy stick
where his left leg, his footballing leg,

had been – taps you on the shoulder
and tells you to go out into the world
with the kind of fire and fearless light only
a child knows, to never give up, to reach
for the stars. Then your uncle performs
his party trick, whirling on the leg

he still has – his fugu a kaleidoscope
of greens and blues – then stopping
on the wooden hoof with a quick bounce.
He does it repeatedly, with flawless timing
and rhythm, drawing a clapping crowd
into a circle around him like a black hole.

星群

［加纳］奈伊·阿伊克维·帕克斯

在父亲家中，他们踩着沙子跳舞
看不上水泥地，被问及原因
他们就说起那个晚上的星斑
在你离开之前

那个晚上，父亲为你张罗一个派对
而你醉生梦死，想跳个尽兴
你的叔叔，一个卸任的维和人员
原来踢球的左腿，已被一支

硬拐替代——他拍着你的肩头
告诉你，出去闯闯吧，带着孩子
才有的蛮劲和无畏，可别放手
去抓摸那些星星。说完
他耍起了绝活，用剩下的一条腿

点地旋转——悲伤与欢乐
都在其中回旋——他又用木腿
回弹，突然停下
一次一次，节奏准确
又明快，众人鼓掌叫好
围拢一圈，好像一个黑洞

He is mystical – half-man, half-beast
as he rears to the syncopated strains of hilife
music; everyone places cedi notes on the pin
board of his forehead and for a moment it is
as though your uncle never grew beyond
the fleet-footed boy he was, never strayed

into the path of a land mine's expletive
volley… But your father, winking, drags
his brother away for a glass of nmɛ daa.
It is only later, when the chairs have been
cleared, and the litter ferreted into bags
that you see it. Your uncle's stick leg

has riddled a constellation of star-like dents
in the pale sand beneath your feet, and looking
up, you note that it is a sepia monochrome copy
of the night sky. Slowly you kneel to touch

a star.

真的好古怪，这个半人半兽
当他打出赫利非的切分曲调。
大家把钱票子纷纷贴在
他脑门上。有一瞬，你的叔叔
仿佛还是那个飞毛腿男孩

从未踏上危机四伏的地雷小路。
但父亲眨了眨眼
用一杯勒姆·达阿酒拖走了弟弟。
最后，当垃圾进袋
椅子擦净，你才看到
叔叔的木腿在你脚下，在细沙上

斑斑点点，已踏出了一个星群。
抬头看，那其实是一份夜空
黯淡的黑白拷贝。缓缓地
你跪下，去抓摸

其中的一颗。

（姜涛　译）

Faith

Nii Ayikwei Parkes

It looked like a landing strip, long corridor of concrete –
rectangular, yet composed of square slabs. Granted,
it was nobody's idea of the centre of excellence it was;
that grey platform muttering with our reluctant footsteps

at 5 a.m., with sleep still scratching at the eyes of the gathered.
From there, we were sent on our four kilometre morning
run, a housemaster waiting with a stopwatch for our return.
But come afternoon, in the wake of siesta, the sun still

harsh above the sandy horizon, ants trailblazing coded patterns
on the edges of the hot stone slabs, we assembled willingly
to live out our dreams. To the left, some triple-jumped
into a world of wild flowers – reds, purples and yellows

blazing beneath their petalled limbs; sprinters exploded
from end to end; footballers juggled and dribbled; while
devotees of the orange bounce – the most recent Michael Jordan-
inspired craze – faked invisible opponents into embarrassing falls.

In the midst of all that, this snapshot: diffused light cannoning
off dust towards the eye, an ethereal tint framing the impossible
profusion of stilled energy – the tamarind tree green in leaf
and ideal for perspective – and in the foreground, me. I am

信心

[加纳] 奈伊·阿伊克维·帕克斯

长长的水泥路面，交错了方格
看上去像一条飞机跑道，假如
这不是出于任何人的精思妙想
那灰色平台呢喃，鼓舞着双脚

早上5点，睡意还粘着眼皮
从那儿起步，我们开始了4公里的晨跑
还有舍监手拿计时器，等我们归来。
但在午后，一觉醒来，太阳依旧

在沙地尽头高高暴晒，灼热的石块旁
蚂蚁排兵布阵，我们自愿集合
想挣脱梦境。向左，接连地跳起
跃入一个野花的世界：红的、紫的、黄的

它们燃烧于绽放中；短跑选手一个冲刺
从头到尾；足球选手运球于足间；
而橘红灌篮手——那迈克尔·乔丹最新
的痴狂——将看不见的对手耍弄

一切的恍惚中，这瞬间的快照：澄清
眼前迷雾缭绕，勾出不可知的
沉静之能的飘忽轮廓——罗望子树枝叶葱绿
高高耸立——在树端，是我，第一次

attempting my first ever back flip. Barefoot, I have flexed
my feet, felt my calves and thighs twitch and engage, swung
my arms fifteen degrees backwards, then suddenly forwards
as I take off, not knowing which part of my body will lead

the renewal of my contact with the ground. There is no mattress,
no coach – just my biology and the concrete. This is how
the camera catches me; suspended in an act of faith, my
back arched instinctively, arms searching the air behind me,

my body drawing a taut line beneath the question:
Do you believe in that which you can not see?

尝试决绝的一跳。我赤足，弯曲了双脚
感到大腿和小腿在紧缩抽搐，向后15度
伸展开双臂，然后突然向前
我起跳了，不知身体的哪一部分

会最先重建与大地的关联。没有床垫
没有教练，只有活生生的肉身。这就是相机
抓拍到的我；悬空于信心，脊背本能地
弯曲，双臂在身后鼓动着空气

一个追问扯紧了我的身子：
"那看不到的东西，你是否相信？"

（姜涛　译）

So it rained…

Obodimma Oha

And the run of water murmurs its hurry to the baffled sand
And the croaking frogs back their threnodies in modest affiliation
And the sky, frowning still, learns to utter softer words
To a softer earth

下雨……

［尼日利亚］奥波多迪玛·奥哈

流水嘟噜着冲向沙堤
呱呱叫的青蛙低唱着庄严的哀歌
天空，微漾的寂静，学会私语情话
向一个更轻柔的大地。

（余旸　译）

Waiting in Shadows

Kofi Anyidoho

I will come with you into Meadows
and watch you wrap your Arms
around Winds
even as the Sun Dances into Twilight.

Then will I Wait for you in Shadows
hold my Breath till Noon
while you Measure our SunGlory
with Flashes of PureDelight
still Rolling in your Eyes.

I will help you gather a Harvest of ButterFlies
still counting gentle murmurs in your Voice
blowing to winds a song of EndlessLonging
searching   forever Searching Horizons
for a lover so long gone into SoulTime.

And when you cross the final path   Beyond our Hope
I will walk back Home with Moon
Counting Stars   still Waiting in Shadows.

在阴影中等待

［加纳］科菲·阿尼多赫

我将和你一起走进牧场
看着你的手臂
缠绕着风
正当太阳跃入黎明的时候。

然后我会在阴影中等你
屏住呼吸一直到正午
当你估量着我们的太阳的光晕
用仍然在你眼中闪动的
瞬间的纯粹喜悦。

我将帮你收集捕获的蝴蝶
仍然细数着你声音中轻柔的喃喃声
吹进风中一首无尽渴望的歌
搜寻着　　永远搜寻着地平线
为一个进入灵歌太久的情人。

当你跨过最后的小径　　离开我们的希望
我将伴着月亮走回家
数着星星　　仍然在阴影中等待。

（张曙光　译）

Over the mounds

Joyce Chigiya

Day in,
I have roamed the country side like mangy dog
going up anthills that sit like sprouting conical heads
only to slip going down the other cheek
bruising my lip from an earthy kiss.

Day out
back on the windy paths again
spacing paces so much I can feel my pair of jeans
threatening to go single on me.
Hand over one ear but that's nothing,
only the cicada's song hitting hard on my drum as it stops,
shoe vanishing into a mound of cow, or is it ox dung
too pissed off to go splitting gender hairs
and some such bullshit!

I have wandered
carried along by the impetus to induce change on my mobile
I have searched these peripheries of the network zone
in vain for that vein of communication
pulsating somewhere around the place where I stay
the place where I so much wanted to live.

粪堆行

［津巴布韦］乔伊斯·齐基娅

白天来了
像一只癞狗，我流浪在乡间
爬上长高的锥形蚁丘
只为了从另一面滑下
粗粗一吻搓伤了我的嘴

白天去了
回到刮风的小路
步履缓慢，我感到双筒牛仔裤
恐将只剩裤腿一条
探了一只耳朵在外，什么听不到
除了知了大声鼓噪
又一脚踏进母牛或公牛的粪堆
满鞋臭屎与脏毛

我游荡着，蠢蠢欲动
揣着手机，在网络上搜索旮旯
最终徒劳，而通话信号
就在某处波动
在这儿的周边
在我渴望的安身之地的周边

（姜涛　译）

The Song of a Twin Brother
—to Kofi Awoonor

Kofi Anyidoho

Stand unshod upon the terrazzo floors of your balcony
Look over the barricade
   to the savanna grasslands of your countryside
Silence the stereo soundz of your radiogram
Open your Soul
   to the mellow tones of your country brother's xylophone

so many Moons ago,
Before our world grew old,
I had a Twin Brother
We sucked the same Breast,
Walked this same Earth,
But dreamt of worlds apart.

And here I am today,
Holding on to Grandfather's sinking boat
While Atsu my Twin Brother
Floats on air in Jumbo Jets
And stares into the skies
And dreams of foreign ports

Atsu e e e!
Atsu e e e!

双胞胎兄弟之歌
　　——给考菲·阿沃诺

[加纳] 科菲·阿尼多赫

赤脚站在你阳台的水磨石地面
越过路障望着
　　　　　　　你乡村的热带大草原
关闭你的立体声收音机
打开你的灵魂
　　　　　　　朝着你乡村兄弟木琴的柔美曲调

太多月亮之前，
在我们的世界变老之前，
我有一个双胞胎兄弟
我们吸吮同一个乳房，
走在这同一片土地，
但梦想的是不同的世界。

今天我在这里，
　　抓住我祖父下沉的小船
而我的双胞胎兄弟阿特苏
飘浮在天上在喷汽客机中
凝视着天空
梦想着外国的港口

阿特苏　噫噫噫！
阿特苏　噫噫噫！

Do not forget the back without which there is no front

Dada is still alive but grown silent
And full of songs sung in a voice
That hints of a heart overstrained
With the burdens of a clan without Elders

Our roof is now a sieve   Atsu
The rains beat us   Beat us
Even in our dreams
And the Gods they say are not to blame.

The State Farms have burnt the thatch and dug its roots
They grow rice.   And cane sugar
But Oh! Atsu
My Twin Brother   Atsu!
Our bowels are not made for the tasty things of life.
The rice   the sugar   all go to Accra
For people with clean stomachs and silver teeth
To eat and expand in their borrowed glory.

Atsu e e e!
Atsu e e e!

I shall give your name to the winds.
They will roam the world for you.

You forget
Atsu   my father's former son

不要忘了过去没有它就没有未来

爹爹仍然活着但变得沉默
唱出的歌都是一种嗓音
暗示着一颗心过于疲惫
由于没有长辈的家族的重负

我们的屋顶现在成了一个筛子　阿特苏
雨敲打着我们　敲打着我们
甚至在我们的梦里
他们说不该去责怪众神。

国营农场烧掉了茅草并连根挖掉
他们种着稻米。还有甘蔗
但哦！阿特苏
我的双胞胎兄弟　阿特苏
我们的肠胃无助于生命中的美味。
稻米　　甘蔗　　全都送到了阿克拉
给有着干净肠胃和银牙的人们
去吃，并在他们窃取的荣誉中膨胀。

阿特苏　噫噫噫！
阿特苏　噫噫噫！

我将把你的名字交给风。
它们将为你在世界上漫游。

你忘记了
阿特苏　　我父亲过去的儿子

You forget the back without which there is no front.

Papa has lost his war against hernia.
Seven Keta market days ago
We gave him back to the soil
And Dada is full of Nyayito songs
sorrowing songs sung in a voice whose echoes
float into the mourning chambers of our soul.

Danyevi leeee!
Dada says
The tasty things of life are good
But
You do not chase Fortune beyond the point
Where Old Sky bends down to have word with Earth.
You do not bury your arm in Fortune's Hole

There have been others before   Atsu
There have been others before you.

Armattoe went away
Came   and went again
Then he never came
Katako too went away
Came   and went again
Then he came. But without his soul.

Atsu
I sit under this Oak where you and I once sat

你忘记了过去没有它就没有未来。

爸爸输掉了对抗疝气的战争。
七个马哈鱼集市日前
我们把他归还给土地
而尼亚依图葬歌充满了父亲的身体
悲伤的歌用一种声音唱出，回声
传进了我们灵魂的服丧间。

丹耶维　哩哩哩!
父亲说
生命中可口的东西很好
但
你不要离开目标去追求财富
那里古老的天空俯身去得到带泥土的词。
你不要把胳膊伸进财富的洞穴

前面还有其它东西　阿特苏
你前面还有其它东西。

阿玛托离开了
来过　　又走了
然后他不再来
卡塔科离开了
来过　　又走了
然后他来了。但是没带灵魂。

阿特苏
我坐在这棵橡树下面，当年我曾和你坐着

and cast cowries in the sand.
I close my eyes. I give your name to the winds
They will roam the world and find your ears.

Fofonyevi leeee!
Papa has gone to Tsyiefe
Dada is full of Nyayito songs
And I   Etse   your Twin Brother
My heart overflows with unsung dirges.

Many many Moons ago
Before the Silence came
I had a Twin Brother.

We shared the same mat
But parted in our Dreams.

在沙滩上扔着贝壳。
我闭上眼睛。我把你的名字交给风
它们将在世界上漫游并找寻你的耳朵。

弗弗恩耶维　哩哩哩!
爸爸已去了特西费
爹爹—肚子尼亚依图葬歌
而我　依特斯　你的双胞胎兄弟
我的心中充溢着没有唱出的哀歌。

很多很多月亮以前
在寂静来临之前
我有一个双胞胎兄弟。

我们分享着同一块垫子
但在我们的梦中分离

（张曙光　译）

V   Hope and the future

African poets find themselves at a point in history, where
the world is shrinking under technology's gigantic reach.
Identities blur as the village poet becomes the seer for a
global search for meaning. As Kenani quotes the Zulu
proverb which articulates the African ethic of universality:
A person is a person because of other people, he invokes
the moral imperative of poets who, in the words of Wole
Soyinka:

> *"Fruits then to your lips: haste to repay*
> *The debt of birth. Yield man-tides like the sea*
> *And ebbing, leave a meaning of the fossilled sands."*

V 希望与前途

    非洲诗人意识到处身于历史的拐点：世界消沉在科技的汪洋大海里。乡村诗人成为环球意识当中的一部分，本地色彩变得模糊不清。克那尼引用祖努谚语来说明非洲伦理之共性：一个人之为一个人概因他人，他唤起诗人道德的迫切性，用沃莱·索因卡之言即为：

> "果子就会在你的嘴边：赶紧偿还
> 出生之债。生出人潮如同大海
> 再退潮，留下亘古不移沙滩的意义。"

Places found in fiction[①]

Chirikuré Chirikuré

every face encountered
the same question
about places I have been to

only the heart answers
the mouth is feeble, but
what is in the heart fills the granary

with dreamy faces, incredulity
they pose more questions of wonder
asking again about where I have journeyed

I answer promptly:
I was in the land of silent echoes
in the sands of the ancient Timbouctou

they shake their heads like bulls
laughing in mockery as they drink:
    such places are only of fiction

---

① Translated from the Shona original, "Nzvimbo
zemumabhuku", by Chenjerai Hove.

虚构的地方①

[津巴布韦] 齐里克热·齐里克热

每一张脸都遇到
同一个问题
关于我曾到过的地方

只有心会回答
嘴巴苍白无力，只有
心中之物能填满谷仓

而他们面带疑惑，如在做梦
提出更多好奇的问题
再次询问我曾旅行何方

我立刻回答：
我曾在静默回音的国土
在古老的通布图城②沙漠中

他们就像牛一样把头直摇
挖苦大笑好像正在喝酒：
这样的地方只属于虚构

---

① 翻译自肖纳部落原创诗歌，名为"Nzvimbo zemumabhuku"，原
作者Chenjerai Hove。原注。
② 此诗译自Timbouctou，通布图，亦称"廷巴克图"。非洲马里共
和国的历史名城，位于撒哈拉沙漠南缘，尼日尔河中游北岸。译注。

I bow my head
consoling my heart with soothing words:
the blessing in the heart is mine

我垂下头
用祥和的话儿安慰我的心：
　　心中的福气是我的福气啊。

（成婴　译）

No boundaries

Keorapetse Kgositsile

I possess neither wings
nor the magician's mischief
but, believe me, I can fly
and I can also be a landscape
of mirrors that name whatever moves
or has pretensions to be alive

On the wingspan of my desire
easy as the approach of any day
you can clearly remember
I can fly to any place
or moment fertile with memory
or create fresh ones without a single boundary
though our lives remain so pathetically prosaic

With informed hope
and resolve we must know
how to move forward to a landscape
where our dreams cannot be turned into nightmare
where our dreams are always in sight
where we must again
redden the blackest folds
of our memory and intent

没有边界

[南非] 凯奥拉佩策·考斯尔

我既无翅膀
也无魔术师的花招
但，相信我，我会飞
我也会成为一片镜中的风景
它命名任何移动的
或配得上活着的事物

以我欲望的翼展
易如你能清晰记得的
任何一天的来临
我能飞到任何地方
任何饱含记忆的时刻
也能创造出新的，无边无际
纵使我们的生活仍如此贫乏

怀着希望和决心
我们必须懂得
怎样移向一片风景
那里我们的梦不会变成梦魇
那里我们的梦始终在望
那里我们必须再次
染红我们记忆和目标的
最黑的褶层

（冷霜　译）

What's the point?

Chirikuré Chirikuré

if it surely takes
a generation's lifetime
chanting emotional slogans
to prove our national manhood
while the love nest is yawning, empty
what then is the point, my dear brothers?

有什么意义？

[津巴布韦] 齐里克热·齐里克热

如果确实花了
一代人一辈子的时间
高喊情绪激昂的口号
来证明我们民族的男子气
而爱巢却哈欠连天，空空如也
那么还有什么意义，我亲爱的兄弟们？

（成婴　译）

The sun, the moon

Beaven Tapureta

The sun, the moon
Have forgotten their foresight
Therefore there will be no tomorrow

Shudder away worry
Look up and smile

The sun, the moon
May remember where they put
Their light

Fight and win
The sun, the moon
Are millenniums old
If they had given up
Under which sky would lovers meet?

太阳，月亮

［津巴布韦］比温·塔普莱塔

太阳，月亮
先见之明忘诸脑后
明日不复明日

抖落烦忧
微笑仰视

太阳，月亮
或许记得光线
抛诸何处

战而胜之
太阳，月亮
千古空悠悠
如果它们放弃
情人幽会何一长空之下？

（韩博　译）

Umuntu Ngumuntu Ngabantu[1]

Stanley Onjezani Kenani

World: a large football pitch
where none is man alone
Life: a game for all, poor or rich
to win they've to play as one

---

[1] Zulu for "Man is man for the people."

UMUNTU NGUMUNTU NGABANTU[①]

[马拉维] 斯坦利·昂热扎尼·克那尼

世界：一个巨大足球场
没有人孤单一人
生命：穷人和富人，是所有人为
赢得自己所扮演角色的一场游戏

（张伟栋　译）

---

① 祖鲁语："人就是人民的人。"原注。

Anthem

Phillippa Yaa de Villiers

Words sketch images on the air.
Voice sets them on fire. I watch traditions
foot stamping, dancing themselves
back to divinity
singing that old song
that we all know as freedom
and a heavy flood bursts
between the chambers of my heart
bright red   vital...

I am alive:
my heart the same size as this fist and I
as little as this finger. We are all connected,
the living and the dead.
We arrive in life and then it
walks away from us;
leaving our bones behind
and our minds are as wide as the universe.
Human evolution began in this corner of the earth,
our ancestors left their dust as chromosomes
in each of us, they made a home,
and hominids stood up as humans and walked
languages fell out of our mouths and talked, walked their way
into and out of landscapes, mindscapes.
We walk in words, creating as we need:

赞美诗

［南非］菲丽帕·维利叶斯

文字凭空勾勒形象。
声音令其着火。我看着传统
踏步逼近，自己跳舞
返回神
歌咏那首我们熟知的
自由之歌
并且一场浩劫洪水喷涌
在我的心房中间
明红色　生机勃勃……

我活着；
我的心拳头般大并且我
如手指般大小。生者和死者
我们都被相连。
我们抵达生命但它
又远离我们。
之后留给我们一片白骨
我们的思想和宇宙一样广阔。
人类的进化从地球的一角开始，
我们的祖先们遗落他们的遗骸像染色体
在我们中的每一个，他们制造巢穴，
类人猿像人一样站立并行走
语言从口中滑落并脱口而出，按他们自己的方式
走进，或走出风景，心境。
我们在词语中行走，当我们需要时我们创造；

we stand shadow-thin

and then

we chase the horizon   disappearing

until   we appear again.

Miracles exist. Victims become heroes:

a man with no legs is the fastest runner in the world.

a woman who cannot walk, swam to golden glory.

Our brains are two halves, reflecting duality,

a system of thinking

in pairs of opposites

like an on-off switch:

like a two way street:

day night wrong right man woman black white

Caster Semenya the intersex athlete

is an invitation

to consider the end of two-way thinking. A provocation

to refine our definition of what it means to be human

or woman. A conundrum. We find ourselves in a hard land

that we don't understand, we've never been here before but

this is what the future looks like. We will have to

stretch our minds from a street

to a field to an ocean to a universe to

accommodate our infinite uniqueness.

Miracles exist; we carve them out of our bodies,

we hammer them out of stone and copper,

we weave them out of desire:

for what the world does not contain

我们站立时如猴子身影
然后
我追逐地平线　消失
直到　　我们再次出现。

奇迹生成。牺牲者变成英雄；
没有腿的男人成为世界最快的赛跑者。
一个不会行走的女人，荣获了游泳金牌。
我们的大脑分两半，沉思的二元性，
以成对的对立物形成的
一套思想体系
像一把开关按钮：
像一条双行道：
昼夜正误男女黑白
卡斯特·瑟门雅，这个阴阳人运动员
是一种怂恿
对于两种思考方式的结束。一个挑衅
来精确到底对男人或女人
什么最重要这个定义。猜不透的难题。我们发现自己生活在
令人不解的坚硬土地上，我们从未来过此地但
这就是未来之景。我们将
从一条街道伸展我们的思想
到一片田野到一片大海到一片宇宙直至
提供出我们人类无限的可能性。

奇迹生长；我们从自己的身躯上雕刻出它们，
我们用石头和铜币击撞它们，
我们以希望编织它们：
由于世界有所不包含的事物

our minds create a home, as long as
we are alive,
our hearts as big as our fists and we
as little as our fingers. We are all connected
the living and the dead,
and our minds
are as wide
as the universe.

只要我们活着
我们就创造一个巢穴，
我的心拳头般大并且我
如手指般大小。生者和死者
我们都被相连。
我们的思想
和宇宙一样
广阔。

（叶美　译）

kuzmas

James Matthews

the greyness of a friday morning
partnered with sudden showers
is dissipated with the welcoming warmth
of dylan's voice
as i walk through the doorway
his greeting wafts me back to another time
where sparkling with the youthfulness
of my years i made another visit to my haven
      kuzmas
the place vibrant with the threads
of conversation
an ambiance of its own making
card players, faces flushed with spirits
scored points as they slammed cards
on a table browned with wine stain
above their heads a naked lady framed
disdainfully gazes into the distance
not impressed by their boisterousness
as the hurrahed points collected
      kuzmas
peter, the fish-and-chips man sits
eyes lost in space thoughts astride
a mean machine embracing the night
roaring away to recklessness long spent
students coupled sit starry-eyed not

库兹马斯

［南非］詹姆斯·马修斯

一个星期五早晨的灰暗
伴随着突如其来的阵雨
被迪兰打招呼的声音中的温暖
驱散
当我走过门道
他的问候使我飘飞到另一个时代
那里闪耀着我青春岁月的
光辉我再一次造访了我的港湾
　　　库兹马斯
这地方振响着会话的
线索
一种它自己造成的气氛
打牌的人，兴奋得脸色发红，
一边计数一边把牌甩在
一张酒迹斑斑的褐色桌子上
在他们上方一个画框中的裸女
轻蔑地凝望着远方
不理会他们的喧闹
不理会他们为得分高而叫好
　　　库兹马斯
彼得，一个卖炸鱼加土豆片的男人坐着
两眼迷失在空中思想走了神
一辆摩托拥抱着夜晚
咆哮着走向鲁莽很久以前
学生成对地坐着他们星星般的眼睛并不

engaged in solving mathematical abstractions
seeing themselves as a whole signifying
lovers wrapped in emotional patterns

       kuzmas

bertie, a gracious host, face radiant with
geniality as his voice dispenses friendship towards
those seated
a feeling of tenderness engendered in an extended
family setting
and i, as time eased past the midnight hour
would appeal to bertie for bottled wine
joining my brothers and sisters grouped around
a tree
to toss a toast to bertie, peter, the fisherman
and the camaradie of the card players

       kuzmas

the ambiance still warms me with the accumulation of
my years

专注于解答数学演算问题
把他们自己看成一个整体意味着
被包装在感情模式里的爱侣
　　库兹马斯
伯提，一个和蔼的东道主，脸上洋溢着
亲切当他的声音将友谊传送给
那些坐着的人
一种温柔的情感产生在了一个
大家庭式的氛围中
而我，在午夜后安逸的时分
会向伯提要瓶装的葡萄酒
和我的兄弟姐妹们一起围坐在
一棵树下
为伯提干杯，为彼得、为渔夫
和打牌者的情谊干杯
　　库兹马斯
这气氛仍旧温暖着我随着我岁月的
积累

（周伟驰　译）

Selvame

Tânia Tomé

Estrelas no chão
deitadas de ventre

Rio incestuoso
onde a noite
tem caroço

Incêndios

Não me salves,
selva-me!

征伐我

[莫桑比克] 塔尼娅·托麦

星星
俯卧在大地上

混沌的河水
夜色
美好而疯狂

燃烧吧

莫管我,
征伐我吧!

（鲁扬　译）

حين أغدو إلهةً

فاطمة ناعوت

سأنزعُ الكُرةَ عن ثوبِها
أنفضُ الخريطةَ
فتسقطُ مخطوطاتُ التاريخِ
وخطوطُ الطولِ والعرضِ والحدودْ،
أوزِّعُ الجبالَ والآبارَ
والذهبَ والنِفطَ والطقسَ والغيماتِ
بالقسطِ،
أمرُّ بريشتي
على الوجوه المُتعَبة
فيذوب البياضُ والسوادُ والصُفرة،
تؤول جميعُها إلى لون المشمش،
ومن الألسنِ أنتزعُ اللغاتِ واللهجات
وأصهرُ في بوتقتي
معجمًا أبيضَ من غير سوء
مصفىً من مفرداتِ الزعلْ،

وقبل أن أستوي على عرشي
أضبطُ زوايا الشمسِ و خطَّ الاستواءْ،
وأعدِّلُ قانونَ المطرْ.
سيصفقُ الصحابُ فيما أقصُ الشَّريط:
سبارتاكوس، جوركي، جيفارا،
وابنة الإسكافي التي فاقَ مَهرُها مَهري،
وفي غمرةِ الفرح أتممُ:
هندسةُ الكونِ وظيفتي!
وعند بدءِ الحرب العالميِّة الثالثة،

354

当我成为女神

［埃及］法蒂玛·纳乌特

我将剥开地球的外衣
重新制图
将昔日的地图抛弃
那些经、纬，边界，
山峰和清泉，还有
黄金，汽油，云彩和天气
均由我重新公平分配，
我将用羽毛拂去
疲惫的面容
让白、黑和黄溶为
杏色一体，
我将弄清各种语言和词汇的发音
清除愤怒的辞藻
在我的熔炉里
提炼出没有邪恶的洁白宝藏，

在我登基之前
我要规定太阳的角度和赤道，
并且调整降雨体系。
当我剪彩，追随者们将为之鼓掌
他们是：斯巴达克斯，高尔基，格瓦拉，
补鞋匠的女儿，她的嫁妆比我的还多。
过分的欢乐使我变得口吃：
宇宙建筑师是我的工作！
在第三次世界大战开始时，

أُطرِقُ برهةً
ثم أعيدُ الكُرةَ سيرتَها الأولى.

我将向下看看
然后将全球调回它昔日的轨迹。

（刘炼，刘宝莱　译）

Unbearable hope

Hama Tuma

Joy-bound I leapt into
    the realm of hope
to dream of light
    with closed eyes.
The cobwebs are gone
and no earth is dug for graves.
Far into the horizon the sunlight
shimmers, a beauty to behold, soft,
the rays enter all hearts, and
melt the hatred away.
There is no fear to face life,
tomorrow, to scan back what is
past.
Desperation flees
the frozen shame disappears
ululations herald joy and birth
gunshots celebrate life and not its end.
Joy-bound I leapt into
the realm of hope, to dream.
And I found the dream painful.

难以承受的希望

［埃塞俄比亚］哈玛·图玛

欢乐地我跳进
　　　　希望的地带
　　　　闭起双眼
梦想着光
蜘蛛网不见了
也不用为了坟墓去挖土。
直到地平线阳光
闪耀着，看见美女，柔软，
光线进入所有的心中，并且
融化了仇恨。
不必恐惧地面对生活，
明天，回顾过去的
一切。
绝望飞逝
冻结的羞愧消失
叫喊宣告喜悦和诞生
开枪庆贺生命并不是终结。
喜悦的跳我跳进
希望之中，去梦想。
我发现了痛苦的梦。

（张曙光　译）

Translations

Tolu Ogunlesi

Nights, and I make journeys
that checkpoints would halt in the daytime.
I go without a map, without calculating distances,
because when the heart is bent on believing a lie,
there is no need for a guide.

Leaving, I plant the Nigerian flag
on a dwindling mountain of beans
wash pepper off my hands and off my pockets,
clap away the droning voices on the TV, in the un-
told stories, the dumb oaf in the fire alarm.

My passport is in my pocket,
but my pocket is hanging on the chair.
To sleep I tell myself lies (I am not going anywhere).
To wake I tell myself the truth (I have not gone anywhere).

In between I am in a world where there is no black or white,
where even the checkpoints offer a loaf or a bottle of wine
for the journey ahead. I search for a back copy of Time
magazine in my Lagos office, answer a few phone calls, messages
I left hanging before my departure. But if I drool (if, not when),
it is not onto a sweaty Lagos pillow, and when I wake
(when, not if), it is to gather half-told stories

翻译

[尼日利亚] 陶鲁·欧冈勒斯

夜里，我从事旅行，
白天会被边防检查站阻挠。
我没带地图，也不测算距离，
因为有心相信一个谎言时
不需要向导。

离开时，我在一大堆正缩小的
豆子上插上尼日利亚国旗，
洗掉手上和口袋里的胡椒，
关掉电视机单调的嗡嗡声，尚未
讲述的故事里，火警中的聋哑痴儿。

我的护照在衣袋里，
而我的衣袋挂在椅子上。
要睡觉我就对自己撒谎（我哪儿都不去），
要醒来我就告诉自己真相（我哪儿都没去）。

两者之间，我处于没有黑白的世界，
甚至那儿的检查站为旅行预备了酒和面包。
我在拉格斯的办公室搜寻一本过期的
时代杂志，接几个电话，离开前我让留言
继续贴着。但如果我流口水（是如果，不是当）
也不是流在汗津津的格拉斯枕头上，当我醒来
（是当，不是如果），就去收集那些半熟的故事

and translate them
into a Swedish I still cannot speak.

并把它们译成
我还不会说的瑞典语。

（丁丽英　译）

Dedication
—for Moremi, 1963

Wole Soyinka

Earth will not share the rafter's envy; dung floors
Break, not the gecko's slight skin, but its fall
Taste this soil for death and plumb her deep for life

As this yam, wholly earthed, yet a living tuber
To the warmth of waters, earthed as springs
As roots of baobab, as the hearth.

The air will not deny you. Like a top
Spin you on the navel of the storm, for the hoe
That roots the forests plows a path for squirrels.

Be ageless as dark peat, but only that rain's
Fingers, not the feet of men, may wash you over.
Long wear the sun's shadow; run naked to the night.

Peppers green and red—child—your tongue arch
To scorpion tail, spit straight return to danger's threats
Yet coo with the brown pigeon, tendril dew between your lips.

Shield you like the flesh of palms, skyward held
Cuspids in thorn nesting, insealed as the heart of kernel—
A woman's flesh is oil—child, palm oil on your tongue

献诗
——给莫雷米，1963

[尼日利亚] 沃莱·索因卡

大地不会与橡子一起嫉妒；粪污的地面
龟裂，不是壁虎的皮裂了，但它掉下来
尝尝泥土是为了死，测一下垂直是为了生

如这白薯，全埋在土中，却是活的块茎
能知水的温暖，它被埋如同源泉，
如同猴面包树的根，如同炉床。

空气不会与你无关。会把你
像只陀螺捻在风暴的肚脐眼，至于锄头
它翻掘丛林是为了给松鼠开条道。

要像黑泥炭一样不老，但只有雨的手指
而不是人的脚，能将你拍打。
常披太阳的影子，赤裸着奔向夜晚。

甜椒有绿有红——孩子——你可以喋舌
去尝蝎尾，吐口水回击危险挑衅
但也要唇含卷须上的露水，与棕鸽一道咕咕叫。

保护自己如同棕榈的叶肉，朝天举起尖牙，
嵌上刺，裹严实如同果核的心脏——
女人的肉体是油——孩子，你舌尖的油

Is suppleness to life, and wine of this gourd
From self-same timeless run of runnels as refill
Your podlings, child, weaned from yours we embrace

Earth's honeyed milk, wine of the only rib.
Now roll your tongue in honey till your cheeks are
Swarming honeycombs—your world needs sweetening, child.

Camwood round the heart, chalk for flight
Of blemish—see? it dawns!—antimony beneath
Armpits like a goddess, and leave this taste

Long on your lips, of salt, that you may seek
None from tears. This, rain-water, is the gift
Of gods—drink of its purity, bear fruits in season.

Fruits then to your lips: haste to repay
The debt of birth. Yield man-tides like the sea
And ebbing, leave a meaning of the fossilled sands.

是生命的柔和所在，而这葫芦里的酒
总是一模一样，流走又注满
就像你重装玩具，孩子，要戒掉它我们拥抱

大地的蜜奶，唯一一根肋骨的酒。
现在把舌头探到蜜中，直到你的脸蛋成为
蜜蜂乱舞的蜂巢——你的世界需要甜上加甜，孩子。

紫檀遍植心的四周，记着要弘扬
瑕疵——明白吗？很清楚！——那是污泥下
的珍宝，就像女神，要让这滋味

在唇边长留，盐，你从泪水中
可找不到，这雨水，是上帝的
礼物——啜饮它的纯洁，时节到了就结果。

果子就会在你的嘴边：赶紧偿还
出生之债。生出人潮如同大海
再退潮，留下亘古不移沙滩的意义。

（席亚兵　译）

367

附

（本集子里有三首诗被不同译者译出，现照录另一版本，供深研者雅鉴）

Going down there

Phillippa Yaa de Villiers ［南非］菲丽帕·维利叶斯

张曙光　译

在那里沉沦

这是一封被烛光遮住的信：
我把它留给所有同样受到
禁闭，痛苦地挤压和分裂的人们。
那些人用双手紧抓住自己
使得他们不会溢出
和渐渐干涸。
恐惧吞噬着希望如同夜晚吞噬着白天
只是留下星星的碎屑。太遥远了
以致无能为力。

我被强奸，六岁，十一岁，十三岁，十七和十九岁
我不知道我受到了强暴，因为
在我出生的地方
爱是被迫的而且
有时是伤害。

人类的弱肉

无法抵御极端的事情。我们在自己周围
建造了自己，用我们的生命造了
一个栖身之所。
当你盖起一座房子，
你小心地安置着窗子；
当你长大，没有了伤口，
从一位幸存者的眼睛
你看到了生命。
强奸是我的面包：我吃。　　我清楚。
然后；　　我清楚　　我吃。
我房子/身体/外形上的标记
是非洲战士的
疤痕的记忆：故意
造成的伤疤，一种身份的符号。
我读着它们像盲文。

当他们找到我时我肮脏，
疯狂，沉默。他们问我：发生了
什么？怜悯打开了
记忆的笼子，落在我身上的话
像格莱特黑暗的森林里的面包屑，
希望的小圆石，
语言变成了灯光
告诉我
如何回到家里。

我现在康复了，
但我看上去
再不相同。

Anthem

Phillippa Yaa de Villiers ［南非］菲丽帕·维利叶斯

周伟驰　译

赞美诗

词语在空气中描画出形象。
声音让它们着火。我看着传统
跺着脚，跳着舞
重又与神灵相通
唱着那首
我们称之为"自由"的老歌
有一股激流爆发
在我的心腔之间
亮红　生机勃勃……

我还活着：
我的心大如这拳头而我
小如这手指。我们彼此相连，
生者和死者。
我们抵达生命然后它
离开我们；
把我们的骨头留在身后
而我们的心像宇宙一般辽阔。
人类的进化开始于地球的这一个角落，

我们的祖先留下他们的尘土一如染色体
在我们每个人身上，他们建了一个家，
而人科动物站立成人并且行走
语言从我们口中飘落并且谈话，走着它们的路
进出于风景，心灵的风景。
我们走进词语，一旦需要就创造：
我们站立着影子单薄
然后
我们追逐地平线　　消失着
直到　　我们重新出现。

奇迹是有的。受害者变成了英雄：
一个没有腿的男人是世界上跑得最快的人。
一个不能走路的女人游泳拿了金牌。
我们的大脑有两半，反映了二元性，
一个以成双的对立面
进行思考的系统
像一个"开关"：
像一条双向街：
白天黑夜错误正确男人女人黑人白人
两性运动员卡斯特·舍门雅
是一个邀请
请我们考虑停止双向思维。是一个刺激
请我们小心定义什么是"人"
或"女人"。一个难题。我们置身在一块艰难的土
地上
对它我们不理解，我们从未到过这里但
看来未来就是这样子。我们将不得不
把我们的心灵从一条街

伸向一片田野一个海洋一个宇宙以
顺应我们无限的独特性。

奇迹是有的；我们从自己身体里把它们雕刻出来，
我们从石头和铜块中把它们敲打出来，
我们从欲望中把它们编织出来；
为世界不能容纳的事物
我们的心灵创造了一个家，只要
我们还活着，
我们的心就大如我们的拳头而我们
小如我们的手指。我们彼此相连
生者和死者，
我们的心灵
跟宇宙一样
辽阔。

Biographies

Ama Ata Aidoo (Ghana) was born in a village in Ghana's Central Region. At the age of 15 she decided that she wanted to be a writer. Aidoo studied literature at the University of Ghana and on graduation, got appointed as Junior Research Fellow in the Institute of African Studies, and later a lecturer at the University of Cape Coast. In January 1982 she was appointed Minister of Education. She resigned 18 months later and moved to Zimbabwe to become a full-time writer. After leaving Zimbabwe, she lived and taught in the USA. She has won many literary awards including the 1992 Commonwealth Writers Prize for Best Book (Africa) for Changes. She is the founding Executive Director of Mbaasem, the Ghanaian and African women writers' foundation, and a Visiting Professor to the Africana Studies Department, Brown University. Aidoo's books include *Our Sister Killjoy*, a novel, and *The Girl Who Can*, a collection of short stories.

Kofi Anyidoho (Ghana) is Professor of Literature, Director of the CODESRIA African Humanities Institute Program, former Ag Director, School of Performing Arts and former Head of the English Department, University of Ghana. His published works include five collections of poetry in English, a children's play in Ewe and English, two CD & cassette recordings of his poetry in Ewe. His GhanaNya CD presents Anyidoho as a poet-singer, his voice alternating with that of his late mother, Abla Adidi Anyidoho, herself a poet-cantor in the Ewe oral tradition. A Fellow of the Ghana Academy of Arts and Sciences and past President of the African Literature Association, he was recently appointed first occupant of the Kwame Nkrumah Chair in African Studies at the University of Ghana.

Shabbir Banoobhai (South Africa) has been a teacher, a university lecturer, and a practising Chartered Accountant. All his published work may be found on his website: www.veilsoflight.com. He is currently working on his first

373

novel. Douglas Livingstone, his mentor, has said of his writing: 'Almost every line of the work was subliminally ignited by the ancient great Islamic poets'; Michael Chapman, of the University of Kwa-Zulu Natal, has remarked: 'A wise, distinctive voice; pure, powerful poetry'.

Joyce Chigiya (Zimbabwe) works as teacher at a rural school in Zimbabwe. When the University of Zimbabwe opened a degree programme for practising teachers at the Masvingo State University, Joyce was part of the pioneer intake. Still in pursuit of poetry, Chigiya's research was an enquiry into the use of verse in the teaching of English as a second language. The result was one very interesting collection of spontaneous verse by young but perceptive potential poets. She was in the 2004-2005 intake of the Crossing Borders Writing Project (Zimbabwe). In 2006 Joyce participated in a cultural exchange with Ugandan poets.

Chirikuré Chirikuré was born in Gutu, Zimbabwe. He is a graduate of the University of Zimbabwe and an Honorary Fellow of Iowa University, USA. A performance poet, he now works for an international development agency as a programme officer for culture and also works as a cultural consultant. Chirikuré has published three volumes of his poetry: Rukuvhute (1989, College Press), Chamupupuri (1994, College Press), Hakurarwi – We Shall not Sleep (1998, Baobab Books). He has also written and translated a number of children's stories and educational books. All of Chirikure's poetry books received first prizes in the annual Zimbabwe writer of the year awards.

Tjawangwa Dema (Botswana) also widely credited as TJ Dema is a Botswana based performance poet, writer, columnist and voice-over artist. She was a 2005/06 participant in the British Council's Crossing Borders project, the 31st Cambridge Seminar on Contemporary Literature as well as serving as mentor to Power in the Voice (PIV) national champions throughout 2007/08. A longstanding member of The Live Poets,

The Writers Association of Botswana and a founding member (alumni) of the acclaimed ELP! collective who have coordinated Botswana's sole annual poetry festival since 2004. TJ Dema recounts as her more memorable performances those in the United Kingdom, India, South Africa as well as Zimbabwe and is "looking forward to sharing word in France, Denmark and the Ukraine later this year".

Dorian Haarhoff is a South African/Namibian poet. A former Professor of English Literature in Namibia he now facilitates creative writing, story-telling and personal and professional development workshops in different parts of the world and acts as a writing mentor. His book, The Writer's Voice, is a collection of reflections and exercises and is one of South Africa's most popular writing manuals. The poetic tradition, zen, mythology, spirituality, whole brain theory, the new Physics, narrative therapy, Eco and Jungian psychology influence his writing. Dorian is working on his seventh collection of poetry. He has been participating poet at Poetry Africa, SA and at the International Poetry Festival in Colombia, South America.
Website: *http://dorianhaarhoffwriter.homestead.com/*

Amanda Hammar is a Zimbabwean professor of African Studies at Copenhagen University. Prior to an academic life, she worked in the newly independent Zimbabwe state and outside it for many years as a development practitioner. But always, she has been drawn to the power of words as a means of both personal and political reflection and transformation. She engages with the world – through research, teaching and writing, through stillness, friendship and creativity – from multiple positions, but first and foremost as an African, and always as a poet. She has only recently 'come out' publicly as the latter. Her work has been featured on the Poetry International website (2009) and included in the collection State of the Nation: Contemporary Zimbabwean Poetry (2009, The Conversation PaperPress, UK).

Stanley Onjezani Kenani is a Malawian writer of both prose (fiction & non-fiction) and poetry who is also an accountant. As poet, Kenani has performed among others at the Arts Alive Festival in Johannesburg and Poetry Africa in Durban, South Africa. Kenani has won several awards in his country for short story writing. He has served as president of the 400 member-strong Malawi Writers Union and also serves as acting treasurer for the Pan African Writers Association (PAWA), a continental body of writers with headquarters in Accra, Ghana. Stanley's collection of poems Slaughterhouse of Sanity is yet to be published. Website: *http://stanleyonjezanikenani.blogspot.com/*

Keorapetse Kgositsile is South Africa's National Poet Laureate. In 1961 Kgositsile was one of the first young members of the African National Congress (ANC) instructed to leave the country by the leadership of the national liberation movement. After a year in Tanganyika (now Tanzania), he got a scholarship to study Literature and Creative Writing in the United States. After his first post at Sarah Lawrence College in New York in 1969, he taught Literature and Creative Writing at a number of universities in the United States and on the African continent. Kgositsile is one of the most internationally acclaimed and widely published South African poets. His poetry collections include My Name is Afrika, Heartprints, To the Bitter End, If I Could Sing, This Way I Salute You. He has been the recipient of a number of literary awards including, the Gwendolyn Brooks Poetry Prize, the Harlem Cultural Council Poetry Award. In 2008 he was awarded the National Order of Ikhamanga Silver (OIS).

Lebogang Mashile (South Africa) is a poet, performer, published author, actress, presenter, producer and columnist. It was while she was studying law and international relations at Wits University in Johannesburg that the desire to work as an artist took hold of her. She is author of two collections of poetry. A Ribbon of Rhythm was published in 2005 and is the winner of the 2006 NOMA Award for Publishing in Africa. Flying Above the Sky was published in 2008.

Website: *www.lebomashile.co.za*

James Matthews is a South African poet, novelist and publisher. He has published five collections of poetry, a novel and a collection of short stories. James opened the first black publishing house and also opened a short-lived art gallery. As an apartheid dissident, he was detained in solitary confinement for three months because of his political poetry. Three of his books were banned and he was denied a passport for twenty-three years. James Matthews has been given an award by the City of Cape Town for his fight against apartheid; a lifetime achievement award from the national arts and culture body. He has been made a freeman of Lehrte and Nienburg (Germany). He is recently working on a memoir based on his spell in detention. James Matthews has been presented with the City of Cape Town Civic Award, for achievements in literature, contributions to journalism and inspirational commitment to the struggle for a non-racial South Africa in 2010.

Keamogetsi Joseph Molapong (Namibia) has been writing poetry since 1990. He was instrumental in establishing the two Windhoek poetry groups Ama Poets and Kitso Poets in 1992 and 1996 respectively, and organised poetry competitions promoted by the publisher New Namibia Books, as well as by the Namibia National Student's Organization (NANSO), and other sponsors. Since 2002 the poet produced a poetry production called *The Black People I Know*, his last poetry productions include. In 2008, through an initiative called Township Productions, Keamogetsi started a poetry publication called POETREE, which up to date has seen 6 Editions. Molapong has published a collection of poetry called Come Talk Your Heart in 2005 and co-edited and contributed to another poetry anthology called In Search of Questions. He has also started working on his second poetry collection called The Scares On My Skin which he plans to publish in 2011.

377

فاطمة ناعوت (**Fatima Naoot**) (Egypt) is considered one of the most re-
markable voices in Arabic poetry. She is a freelance writer. Writes 4 constant
weekly columns in Egyptian and Arabic noted newspapers. Born in Cairo,
she graduated in 1987 from the faculty of Engineering, Architecture depart-
ment, at Ein Shams University, Cairo. She has published 16 books to date: six
poetry collections, seven translated anthologies from English into Arabic, and
three books of criticism. She has translated into Arabic the novels and stories
of: Virginia Woolf, John Ravenscroft (Britain), Chimamanda Nagozi Adichie
(Nigeria), and dozens of British and American contemporary poets. She won
the first prize of the "Arabic Poetry 2006" competition in Hong Kong for her
fifth poetry collection, A Bottle of Glue, a Chinese/English edition (Nadwah
Press, 2007). She participated in most noted international poetry festivals
round the world, presenting the name of Egypt, and her poetry has been
translated into: English, French, German, Italian, Turkish, Dutch, Spanish,
Chinese, Hebraic, Persian, and Kurdish.

Tolu Ogunlesi (Nigeria): Ogunlesi has contributed to a number of
literary journals including The London Magazine, World Literature
Today, Wasafiri, and Stanford's Black Arts Quarterly, among others.
He is the author of the collection of poetry Listen to the geckos sing-
ing from a balcony (Bewrite Books, 2004). In 2007 he was awarded a
Dorothy Sargent Rosenberg poetry prize, in 2008 the Nordic Africa In-
stitute (Sweden) Guest Writer Fellowship, and in 2009 a Cadbury Visit-
ing Fellowship by the University of Birmingham, England. He lives in
Lagos, Nigeria, and works as Features Editor with a daily newspaper.
Website: *http://toluogunlesi.wordpress.com/*

Obododimma Oha (Nigeria) teaches Stylistics and Semiotics in the Depart-
ment of English at the University of Ibadan in Nigeria. His poems have ap-
peared in journals such as Otoliths, Shadowtrain, Postcolonial Text, African

378

Writing Online, Sentinel Poetry Online, Agenda, Portal, Ekleksographia, Envoi, 2009 Poetry Almanac, FoggedClarity, and Assisi. With Anny Ballardini, he co-edited While the He/Art Pants, an online anthology of Poetic responses to the 2008 America elections and another anthology on Health & Illness. Website: *http://udude.wordpress.com/*

Nii Ayikwei Parkes (Ghana) is a former International Writing Fellow at the University of Southampton and a 2007 recipient of Ghana's ACRAG award for poetry and literary advocacy. He has been writer-in-residence at the Poetry Café (London) and California State University, Los Angeles and has performed poetry all over the world at festivals such as the Lancaster Literature Festival and the Austin International Poetry Festival. In 2009, Nii's short story, 'Socks Ball', was highly commended in the Caine Prize for African Writing, and his novel 'Tail of the Blue Bird' was shortlisted for the 2010 Commonwealth Writers' Prize.

www.niiparkes.com

Shailja Patel is a Kenyan poet, playwright and activist, who trained as a political economist, accountant, and yoga teacher. Her one-woman show, Migritude toured globally to critical acclaim, and closed the Nairobi World Social Forum. The bilingual Italian-English edition of Migritude, published by Lietocolle,was shortlisted for the Camaiore International Poetry Prize. An expanded US edition is forthcoming in 2010 from Kaya Press.

Honours include a Sundance Theatre Fellowship, Ford Foundation Commission, Voices of Our Nations Poetry Award, Lambda Slam Championship, and the Outwrite Poetry Prize.Shailja was 2009 African Guest Writer at Sweden's Nordic Africa Institute. Her work has been translated into13 languages. Website: *www.shailja.com*

Wole Soyinka was born Abeokuta, near Ibadan/ Nigeria. After preparatory university studies in 1954 at Government College in Ibadan, he continued at the University of Leeds, where, later, in 1973, he took his doctorate. During the six years spent in England, he was a dramaturgist at the Royal Court Theatre in London 1958-1959. In 1960, he was awarded a Rockefeller bursary and returned to Nigeria to study African drama. At the same time, he taught drama and literature at various universities in Ibadan, Lagos, and Ife, where, since 1975, he has been professor of comparative literature. In 1960, he founded the theatre group, "The 1960 Masks" and in 1964, the "Orisun Theatre Company", in which he produced his own plays and took part as actor. He has periodically been visiting professor at universities of Cambridge, Sheffield, and Yale. During the civil war in Nigeria, Soyinka appealed in an article for cease-fire. For this he was arrested in 1967, accused of conspiring with the Biafra rebels, and was held as a political prisoner for 22 months until 1969. While in prison he wrote poetry on tissue paper which was published in a collection titled Poems from Prison. He writes in English and his literary language is marked by great scope and richness of words. He won the Nobel Prize in Literature in 1986, the first African to be so honoured. In 1994, he was designated United Nations Educational, Scientific and Cultural Organization (UNESCO) Goodwill Ambassador for the promotion of African culture, human rights, freedom of expression, media and communication.

Véronique Tadjo (Côte d'Ivoire) was born in Paris, France, but was brought up in Abidjan, Ivory Coast. She has a doctorate in African American Literature and Civilization from the Sorbonne. She has travelled extensively in Africa, Europe and the United States. Tadjo has conducted writing workshops in several countries. She has published two collections of poems. Her novel Reine Pokou [Queen Pokou] was awarded the prestigious literary Prize "Grand Prix Littéraire d'Afrique Noire" in 2005. After spending a few years in Kenya and in England, she now lives in South Africa where she is Head of French Studies at the University of the Witwatersrand in Johannesburg.

Website: *www.veroniquetadjo.com*

Beaven Tapureta was born in Chitungwiza, Zimbabwe. From 2003 to 2009, he was Programme Officer for BWAZ. A poet, creative writer, and literary journalist, Tapureta belongs to the new generation of writers in Zimbabwe. He was nominated for the 2009 National Arts Merit Awards (NAMA) – Zimbabwe - in the Print Media category. Tapureta features in the poetry publication State of the Nation: Contemporary Zimbabwean Poetry (2009, Conversation Paper Press, UK). His story 'Cost of Courage' will appear in the forthcoming anthology African Roar (Lion Press and StoryTime, 2010) in the UK. Tapureta is the founder of a writers' organization called Writers International Network Zimbabwe.

Website: *http://storytime-beaven-tapureta.blogspot.com/*
and *http://win-zimbabwe.blogspot.com*

Alemu Tebeje Ayele, born in Ethiopia, did his undergraduate studies in Ethiopian Languages and Literature at the Addis Abeba University. After working for the Ethiopian Science and Technology Commission as a public relation officer & editor for 5 years, he came to the UK in 1991 to complete his postgraduate studies in Journalism at the University of Wales. Since then he is working as a community activist, freelance writer and editor.

Tânia Tomé (Mozambique) is a singer, composer, poet, presenter, actress, producer and published author. An early passion for the arts, music and singing culminated in her winning the first prize, at the age of seven, for best voice in an international competition organised by the World Health Organization in Mozambique. With the conclusion of her degree in economics, Tomé won the Mario Soares Foundation of Portugal award for academic commitment in combination with social-artistic activities. She produced and published the first DVD of poetry in Mozambique: "Showesia" is her concept, movement and spectacle. Tomé works as well as a head of department of credit and risk mitigation in a financial instituion in Mozambique.

Website: *www.showesia.com*

Hama Tuma is an Ethiopian writer and poet born in Addis Abeba. He has published two poetry collections in English (Of Spades and Ethiopians and Eating an American and other Poems), two poetry collections in Amharic (Habeshigna 1 and Habeshigna II) , a novel in Amharic (Kedada Chereka) two short story collections in English (The Case of the Socialist Witchdoctor and Other Stories/now translated into Hebrew and published in Israel/ and The Case of the Criminal Walk and Other Stories). He has also written three volumes of satirical articles on Africa and the world under the general title of African Absurdities of which volume one has been translated into French and Italian. Hama Tuma continues to write poems (mostly in Amharic these days) and newspaper articles in English for magazines.

Website: *www.hamatuma.com*

The South African performance poet and actress **Phillippa Yaa de Villiers** is winner of the National Arts Festival/de Buren Writing beyond the Fringe Prize 2009. She also received Honourable Mention (2009) and Highly Commended (2010) for her haiban from the Kikakuza Haiban Society in Japan, and was shortlisted for the Pen/Studinski Prize 2009. She wrote and performed Original Skin at the Market Theatre and the National Arts Festival in Grahamstown and at the Humboldt University literary conference Conventions and Conversions in Berlin in 2010,. She has published two collections of poetry Taller than Buildings (2006) and The Everyday Wife (Modjadji, 2010). She worked as a scriptwriter for television and radio for ten years, and studied at the Jacques Lecoq International Theatre School in Paris, Rhodes University and Wits University.

Website: *www.phillippayaadevilliers.org*

Makhosazana Xaba is a South African poet who has published two books of poetry: these hands (Timbila, 2005) and Tongues of their Mothers (UKZN Press, 2008). Her short stories, essays and poetry have appeared in many anthologies.

She regularly writes profiles of women artists, poets, playwrights, film makers and writers for the South African Labour Bulletin and is writing a biography of Noni Jabavu. Her four children's books were published by Nutrend Publishers. In 2005 she won the Deon Hofmeyr Award for Creative Writing for her then unpublished short story, Running. She holds a Diploma in Journalism (with distinction) from the Werner Lamberz International Institute of Journalism and an MA in Writing (with distinction) from the University of the Witwatersrand. She has a long history for feminist activism, specialized in women's health.

诗人小传

　　阿玛·阿塔·艾杜（加纳）出生于加纳中央范特语区的一个小村子。她的父亲创办了村子里的第一家学校，对她影响很大。十五岁的时候，她就想成为一名作家，不到四年就实现了她的抱负。她受到鼓励去参加一家报纸的短篇小说赛，直到在报纸上看到她的名字才知道自己赢了。艾杜在加纳大学读过文学，后成为大学讲师。1982年1月她被任命为教育部长。在任时艾杜想在加纳实现全民免费教育——但18个月后她就认识到这个目标无法实现，就此辞职。她移居津巴布韦，成了专职作家，也在美国居住、任教。她获得过很多文学奖，其中《变化》曾获得1992年的联邦作家最佳书籍奖（非洲）。她的著作还有长篇小说《搅局姐妹》及短篇小说集《无所不能的女孩》。

　　科菲·阿尼多赫（加纳）是文学教授，非洲社会科学研究发展会的负责人，曾任表演艺术学院先锋艺术院长，加纳大学英语系主任。他出版有五本英语诗集，一本用埃维语和英语写成的儿童剧本，两张他用埃维语朗读自己诗歌的CD和磁带。在CD《加纳尼雅》里，他是一个诗人歌唱家，和他逝去的母亲，埃维语口头传统歌手，阿布拉·阿迪迪·阿尼多赫的声音交替出现。他是加纳艺术科学院的研究员，曾担任非洲文学会的主席，最近被任命为加纳大学第一任夸姆·茹玛非洲研究专业的主任。

　　沙比尔·巴努海（南非）曾做过教师，大学讲师，执业的特许会计师。他的全部作品可以在其网站上找到：www.veilsoflight.com。他正在写他的第一部小说。他的导师道格拉斯·利温斯通这样评价他的写作："几乎每一行都在潜意识里被伟大的古代伊斯兰诗人点燃"。夸—祖鲁·纳塔尔大学的麦克·贾普曼对他的评价："一个智慧的、与众不同的声音；纯粹、强力的诗歌。"

乔伊斯·齐基娅（津巴布韦）在津巴布韦一个农村学校做老师。津巴布韦大学曾在马斯温格州立大学开办过一个授予执业教师学位的专业，乔伊斯是最早被录取的一员。在其诗歌生涯里，齐基娅探索了将诗歌运用于英语作为非母语的教学中，其结果编入一本很有趣的集子里，里边收的都是年轻而才华初显的诗人的诗。她是2004—2005年度的跨地域写作计划（津巴布韦）的成员。2006年乔伊斯参加了一个和乌干达诗人的文化交换活动。

齐里克热·齐里克热出生于津巴布韦的谷图。他毕业于津巴布韦大学，曾获得美国爱荷华大学的荣誉研究员。作为一个表演诗人，他在一家国际发展中心主管文化，兼文化咨询员。齐里克热出版过三卷诗集：*Rukuvhute*（1989，学院出版社），*Chamupupuri*（1994，宝巴书局），*Hakurarwi － We Shall not Sleep*（1998，宝巴书局）。他还写作并翻译过过一些儿童故事和教育方面的书，每一本都获得了津巴布韦年度作家的头等奖项。

贾旺娃·迪玛（博茨瓦纳）是基于博茨瓦纳的表演诗人，作家，专栏作家，配音艺术家，被广泛称为TJ迪玛。她2005/06年参与英国文化协会的"跨国界项目"，第31届剑桥当代文学研讨会，并于2007/08年出任"声音中的力量"的顾问。她是"活着的诗人"以及博茨瓦纳作家协会的长期成员，著名的ELP的创始人，从2004年起举办博茨瓦纳年度诗歌节。TJ迪玛在英国，印度，南非以及津巴布韦举办过令人难忘的表演，并将于下半年去法国，丹麦和乌克兰交流。

多利安·哈尔霍夫是南非/纳米比亚诗人。曾在纳米比亚做过英语文学教授，现在在世界各地的一些工作室从事关于创造性写作，故事讲述，以及个人和职业发展的工作，任写作顾问。他的《作家的声音》是一本反思、练习集，是南非最受欢迎的写作手册之一。他所受的影响来自于诗歌传统，禅，精神性，全脑理论，新物理学，故事疗法，生态心理学和荣格心理学等等。多利安正在写第七本诗集。他参加过南非非洲诗人协会，南美哥伦比亚国际诗歌节。

网址：http://dorianhaarhoffwriter.homestead.com/

阿曼达·哈玛是哥本哈根大学的非洲研究教授，津巴布韦人。在从事学术生涯前，她在新独立的津巴布韦政府及民间做过很多年的发展工作。但她最执着的还是文字作为个人和政治的反思转变力量。她从多个角度和世界发生关系——通过研究，教学，写作，通过静止，友谊和创造性，但最重要的还是她的非洲身份，而诗人是她永久的角色。她只是在最近才以其诗人身份面向公众。她的作品发表在"国际诗歌"网站上（2009），收入《国家状态：当代津巴布韦诗歌》（2009，英国对话出版社）。

斯坦利·昂热扎尼·克那尼是马拉维作家，写散文（小说与非小说）和诗歌，同时还是一个会计师。作为诗人，克那尼曾在南非约翰内斯堡的艺术节和德班的非洲诗活动中进行表演。克那尼曾在他的国家获得几个短篇小说奖，还曾担任马拉维的成员达400人之多的作家联合会的主席，总部位于加纳阿克拉的泛非作家协会的代理财务主管。斯坦利的诗集《理智的屠宰场》即将出版。

网址：http://stanleyonjezanikenani.blogspot.com/

凯奥拉佩策·考斯尔是南非的国家桂冠诗人。在1961年国民解放运动领导人指示下撤离的非洲国民议会党的成员中，考斯尔是其中最年轻的一个。在坦噶尼卡（现坦桑尼亚）逗留一年后，他获得了美国的一个文学研究和创造性写作的奖学金。1969年在萨拉·劳伦斯学院获得他的第一个教职，此后他在美国和非洲大陆的一些大学教文学和创造性写作。考斯尔是南非最受国际推崇的诗人，著述颇多。他的诗集有《我的名字是非洲》，《心印》，《痛苦结局》，《假如我能唱》，《我这样赞颂你》等等。他是一系列文学奖的获得者，包括格温道恩·布鲁克斯诗歌奖，哈莱姆文化协会诗歌奖。2008年他获得了伊南非总统颁发的伊卡曼加国家银质勋章。

386

勒布干·马希尔（南非）是一个诗人，表演家，作家，女演员，主持人，制作者和专栏作家。在约翰内斯堡的维茨大学学法律和国际关系的时候，她有了成为一个艺术家的想法。她出版过两本诗集。《一个节奏的丝带》出版于2005年，获得2006年的非洲NOMA出版奖。《在天空中飞翔》出版于2008年。

网址：www.lebomashile.co.za

詹姆斯·马修斯是南非诗人，小说家和出版人。他出版有五本诗集，一部小说和一个短篇小说集。詹姆斯开办了第一家黑人出版社，还开办过一家短命的画廊。作为一个种族隔离政策的不同意见者，他曾因其政治诗被单独关押过三个月。他的三本书被禁，长达二十三年被拒绝发给护照。詹姆斯·马修斯因其散文写作在对种族主义政权的斗争中所作的贡献获得过开普顿市颁发的一个奖项，还获得过国家艺术文化机构的终身成就奖，以及德国最知名人文杂志《勒赫特》与纽伦堡市颁发的自由人奖。他最近在写一本回忆录，是关于他在拘留期间的厄运的。2010年詹姆斯·马修斯获得开普敦市民奖，表彰他的文学成就，对新闻业的贡献以及为争取一个非种族主义南非所作的鼓舞人心的献身。

齐莫格茨·约瑟夫·莫拉庞（纳米比亚）从1990年开始写诗。他对1992年和1993年成立于韦德和克的阿玛诗人和季佐诗人组织起了关键作用，他组织了由新纳米比亚书局、纳米比亚民族学生会和其他组织赞助的诗歌竞赛。2002年他制作了诗剧《我知道的黑人》。2008年他通过一个叫做"小镇制作"的倡议，开始出版《诗人树》，迄今已出到第六版。莫拉庞在2005年出版了一本诗集《来说你的心》，合作编辑并出版诗歌选集《追寻问题》。他正在写他的第二本诗集《我皮肤上的伤疤》，计划于2011年出版。

法蒂玛·纳乌特（埃及）被认为是阿拉伯诗歌中最值得注意的声音。她是一个自由写作人。她为埃及语和阿拉伯语的报纸撰写四个每周专栏。她生于开罗，1987年毕业于开罗的艾因·沙姆斯大学建筑系的工程专业。迄今她出版了16本书：6本诗歌集，7本从英语翻译到埃及语的选集，3本批评。她把弗吉尼亚·伍尔夫，约翰·雷文斯克罗福特（英国），施玛曼达·纳高斯·阿迪施（尼日利亚），和许多英国、美国当代诗人的小说和短篇故事翻译成阿拉伯语。她的第五本诗集《一瓶胶水，中英对照版》（纳德瓦出版社2007）获得2006年香港阿拉伯诗歌竞赛的一等奖。她参加过全世界很多著名的诗歌节，宣扬埃及，她的诗歌被翻译成以下语言：英语，法语，德语，意大利语，土耳其语，西班牙语，中文，希伯来语，波斯语和库尔德语。

陶鲁·欧冈勒斯（尼日利亚）给很多文学期刊写过稿，包括《伦敦杂志》，《今日世界文学》，《瓦萨费里》和《斯坦福黑人艺术季刊》等等。他著有诗集《听蜥蜴在阳台上唱歌》（比莱特书局，2004）。2007年他获得了多萝西·萨尔金特·罗森博格诗歌奖，还有2008年的北欧非洲学院（瑞典）客座作家奖金，2009年英国伯明翰大学的坎特伯雷访问学者奖金。他住在尼日利亚的拉各斯，在一家日报社做专题编辑。

网址：http://toluogunlesi.wordpress.com/

奥波多迪玛·奥哈（尼日利亚）在尼日利亚伊巴丹大学英语系叫文体学和符号学。他的诗出现在《耳石》《阴影火车》《后殖民文本》《非洲写作在线》《森提诺诗歌在线》《议程》《门户》，Ekleksographia，《使节》《2009诗歌年鉴》《起雾的清晰》，Assisi 等刊物。他和安妮·巴拉尔第尼合作编辑了《当心在跳》，一本对2008年美国选举的诗歌回应的网上选集，还有另一本关于健康和疾病的选集。

奈伊·阿伊克维·帕克斯（加纳）是南安普顿大学的前写作指导，2007因其诗歌和文学活动年获得加纳的ACRAG奖。他曾任诗歌咖啡馆（伦敦）的驻馆作家，和洛杉矶加州州立大学的驻校作家，在世界各地举办的诗歌节上表演诗歌，如兰开斯特文学节，奥斯汀国际诗歌节。2009年奈伊的短篇小说《袜球》得到凯恩非洲写作奖的高度赞扬，他的小说《蓝鸟的尾巴》入围2010年的联邦作家奖。

网址：www.niiparkes.com

莎尔遮·佩特尔是肯尼亚诗人，剧作家和活动家，是受过训练的政治经济学家，会计师，瑜伽教练。她的独女秀《移民》在全球巡回演出，广受好评，在内罗毕世界社会论坛上是压轴戏。在利特克勒出版社出版的意英双语版的《移民》入围卡马约雷国际诗歌奖。美国扩充版即将由卡亚出版社于2010年出版。荣誉包括圣丹斯戏剧奖，福特基金会资助，民族声音诗歌奖，兰姆达·斯莱姆大赛，以及写诗进步奖。莎尔遮是2009年度的瑞典北欧非洲学院的客座作家。她的作品被翻译成13种语言。

沃莱·索因卡出生在尼日利亚的伊巴丹市附近的阿贝奥库塔。1954年经过在伊巴丹的政府学院的预备学习，他进入利兹大学，并于1973年拿到博士学位。在英格兰的六年期间，他担任过伦敦皇家宫廷剧院的戏剧顾问（1958—1959）。1960年他获得洛克菲勒资助，回到尼日利亚研究非洲戏剧。他同时还在伊巴丹，拉各斯，伊费大学教戏剧和文学。从1975年起，他在伊费大学做比较文学教授。1960年他创办了"1960年的面具"剧团，1964年创办了"奥利桑戏剧公司"，演出他自己的戏，自己扮演角色。他定期去剑桥，谢菲尔德，和耶鲁大学做访问教授。尼日利亚内战期间，他在一篇文章里呼吁停战。因此在1967年被捕，被指控和比夫拉叛军勾结，作为政治犯一直到1969年，整整22个月。他在狱中时在面巾纸上写诗，出有诗集《狱中诗》。他获得1986年诺贝尔文学奖，是第一个获得此奖的非洲人。1994年他被委派为联合国教科文组织的亲善大使，促进非洲文化，人权，言论、媒体以及交流自由。

伏罗尼克·塔乔（科特迪瓦）生于法国巴黎，在科特迪瓦（象牙海岸）的阿比让长大。她获得索邦大学的非裔美国文学和文化的博士学位。曾周游非洲，欧洲和美国。塔乔在好几个国家主持过写作班。她出版过两本诗集，小说《波库女王》在2005年获得令人尊敬的"黑非洲文学大奖"。她曾在肯尼亚和英国生活,现在住在南非,担任约翰内斯堡的维特沃特斯兰德大学法国研究主任。

比温·塔普莱塔生于津巴布韦的齐通维扎。从2003年到2009年他担任"津巴布韦崭露头角作家协会"的项目负责人。塔普莱塔是一个诗人,创造性写作作家,文学记者,属于津巴布韦的新一代作家。2009年他被提名印刷类的国家艺术优秀奖。他还出现在《国情:当代津巴布韦诗歌》(2009,英国对话出版社)一书中。他的短篇《勇气的代价》将发表于即出的选集《非洲呼啸》(2010,狮子出版社以和《故事时代》杂志)。塔普莱塔是一个作家组织"津巴布韦作家国际网络"的创始人。

网址: http://storytime-beaven-tapureta.blogspot.com/,

http://win-zimbabwe.blogspot.com

阿莱姆·特伯热·艾尔生于埃塞俄比亚,本科在亚的斯亚贝巴大学学埃塞俄比亚语言文学。在埃塞俄比亚科学技术委员会做公共关系专员、编辑五年之后,他于1991年赴英国威尔士大学完成他的新闻学研究生学业。此后他成为一个社区活动家,自由作家和编辑。

塔尼娅·托麦(莫桑比克)是一个歌手,作曲家,诗人,主持人,演员,制作人和出过书的作者。七岁的时候,她对艺术、音乐以及歌唱的热情使她获得了世界卫生组织在莫桑比克举行的一个国际比赛的最佳嗓音头等奖。拿到经济学学位后,托麦获得了葡萄牙的马里奥·索莱斯基金会提供的奖金,从事学术事业及社会艺术活动。她制作出版了莫桑比克的第一个诗歌DVD《Showesia》。托麦在莫桑比克的一家金融机构担任信用及风险管理部门的负责人。

网址: www.showesia.com

哈玛·图玛是埃塞俄比亚作家,诗人,出生于亚的斯亚贝巴。他出版有两本英语诗集(《关于黑桃和埃塞俄比亚人》,《吃一个美国人和其他诗》),两本阿姆哈拉语诗歌集(Habeshigna I,Habeshigna

II），一本阿姆哈拉语小说，两个英语短篇小说集（《社会主义巫医的案例和其他故事》《越线之罪的案例和其他故事》）。他还写了三卷标题为《非洲荒诞经》的关于非洲及世界的讽刺文章，其中第一卷被翻译成法语和意大利语。哈玛·图玛还在继续写诗（大部分用阿姆哈拉语），也给杂志写英文文章。

菲丽帕·维利叶斯是南非表演诗人和演员，2009年国家艺术节边缘之外写作奖的获得者。她还得到了日本俳文社的荣誉提名奖（2009）和强烈推荐奖(2010)，以及2009年度国际笔会斯特金斯基奖。她写作了剧本《旧皮》，并在以下场所亲自表演：市场剧院，格雷厄姆斯敦的国家艺术节，以及洪堡大学文学传统会议，2010柏林文学年会。她还出版了两本诗集《高于建筑》（2006）和《琐屑主妇》（2010，莫加基出版社）。她给电视电台写了十年剧本，曾在巴黎亚克斯·勒克克国际剧院学校，罗兹大学，维茨大学求学。

网址：www.phillippayaadevilliers.org

马克霍萨萨纳·萨巴是南非诗人，出版有两本诗集《这些手》（2005，提姆比拉出版社）和《母亲之舌》（2008，UKZN出版社）。她的短篇小说，散文和诗歌出现在很多选本里。她经常为《南非劳动简报》写关于妇女艺术家，诗人，剧作家，电影制作人以及作家们的传略，正在写诺尼·贾巴乌的传记。她在新浪潮出版社出过四本儿童书。2005年因其尚未出版的短篇小说《跑》获得了迪奥恩·霍夫迈尔创造性写作奖。她获得了沃尔纳·兰波茨国际新闻学院的学士学位，维特沃特斯兰德大学的写作硕士（优秀毕业生）。她长期从事女权活动，专长是妇女健康。

Editors

Phillippa Yaa de Villiers was born in her native city of Johannesburg in 1966, studied in the Eastern Cape and Paris and has worked in the USA and various European countries, Singapore and Hong Kong. She worked as a television writer for ten years before publishing poetry in two collections and a number of journals. She lives in Johannesburg and earns her living as a writer, writing coach and performer.
Website: *www.phillippayaadevilliers.org*

Isabel Ferrin-Aguirre (1978, Berlin / Germany) has studied Spanish, English, Italian Literature in Berlin / Germany, Salamanca// Spain and Cagliari/ Italy. She works as freelance event manager at Poetry Festival Berlin,Literaturwerkstatt Berlin since 2005 and at Haus der Kulturen der Welt since 2010. She worked for the international poetry platform www.lyrikline.org until 2010, culminating in a festival week which was inaugurated by the former German president Horst Köhler. Isabel also works as Spanish / German translator. She has collaborated in the anthologies "VERSschmuggel" 2006 (Spanish- German), 2007 (French – English– German), 2008 (Portuguese – German), 2009 (Arabic – German).

Xiao Kaiyu was born in 1960 in Sichuan province, China, has published several volumes of poetry, spent a number of years in Germany and now lives in the central Chinese city of Kaifeng, and in Beijing.

编者小传

菲丽帕·维利叶斯，1966年生于南非本土城市约翰内斯堡，就学于东开普和巴黎，曾在美国和多个欧洲国家、新加坡和香港工作。他在出版两本诗集和多种报道之前，曾为电视台工作10年。现居约翰内斯堡，作为作家、写作辅导员和表演艺术家而谋取生计。

网址：www.phillippayaadevilliers.org

伊莎贝尔·阿闺热（1978年生于德国柏林）曾在德国柏林、西班牙萨拉曼卡和意大利卡利亚里学习西班牙、英国及意大利文学。从2005年开始，作为不固定的项目负责人为柏林文学馆的国际诗歌节工作；从2010年开始，她同时为德国世界文化宫工作。在2010年之前，她还曾效力于国际诗歌网站www.lyrikline.org，该网站在一个诗歌周受到德国前总统科勒的夸奖。伊莎贝尔是一位西班牙语-德语翻译。她与别人合作翻译了诗文选集*VERSschmuggel*，2006年出版了西班牙-德语对照本，2007年出版了法语-英语-德语对照本，2009年出版了阿拉伯语-德语对照本。

萧开愚，1960年生于四川，曾住柏林，现居开封和北京。出版过诗集数种。

图书在版编目（CIP）数据

这里不平静：非洲诗选：中、法、葡、阿拉伯文、英文／
（南非）维利叶斯，（德）阿闺热，（中）萧开愚编著．
—北京：世界知识出版社，2010.8

ISBN 978-7-5012-3895-8

Ⅰ．①这… Ⅱ．①维…②阿…③萧… Ⅲ．①诗歌—作品
集—非洲—现代—汉语、法文、葡萄牙文、阿拉伯文
Ⅳ．①I402.5

中国版本图书馆CIP数据核字（2010）第148447号

图字：01-2010-5020号

责任编辑	席亚兵
文字编辑	侯福龙
封面设计	小　月
责任出版	赵　玥
责任校对	陈可望

书　　名	**这里不平静——非洲诗选** Zheli Bu Pingjing—Feizhou Shixuan
主　　编	［南非］菲丽帕·维利叶斯　　［德国］伊莎贝尔·阿闺热 ［中国］萧开愚
出版发行	世界知识出版社
地址邮编	北京市东城区干面胡同51号（100010）
网　　址	www.wap1934.com
电　　话	010-65265923（发行）　　010-65233645（书店）
印　　刷	北京盛通印刷股份有限公司
经　　销	新华书店
开本印张	880×1230毫米　1/32　13¼印张
字　　数	273千字
版次印次	2010年8月第一版　2010年8月第一次印刷
标准书号	ISBN 978-7-5012-3895-8
定　　价	48.00元